AS I WALK WITH SPIRIT

Hypnotherapy, Past Lives,

Healing and Spirituality

Mike Wells

RB

Rossendale Books

Simon.

Have a wonderful Christmas.

Published by Lulu Enterprises Inc.
3101 Hillsborough Street
Suite 210
Raleigh, NC 27607-5436
United States of America

Published in paperback 2015
Category: Self-Improvement

ISBN: 978-1-326-02697-4

DISCLAIMER AND/OR LEGAL NOTICES: The information presented herein represents the view of the author as of the date of publication. Because of the rate of which the conditions change, the author reserves the right to alter and update his opinion based on the new conditions. The report is for information purposes only.

While every attempt has been made to verify the information in this book, either the author or his affiliates or partners assume any responsibility for errors, inaccuracies or omissions. Any slights of people or organisations are unintentional. If advice concerning medical or related matters is needed, the services of a fully qualified professional should be sought. This book is not intended as a source of medical advice. Any reference to any person or business whether living or dead is purely coincidental.

ABOUT THE AUTHOR

Mike is a Master Hypnotherapist/Psychotherapist and a PSTEC Master practitioner based in the UK. For over thirty four years he has been helping people overcome all kinds of issues.

It was in 1984 that he also became very involved in Spirituality and over the years he has experienced many things that helped him and others on their journey. He is an expert on Past Life Regressions and has assisted hundreds of people to experience one. He shares with you parts of his actual case histories and experiences using spiritual energy. He gives you an insight into his journey throughout the years with many testimonials and suggestions included.

Now in his early sixties, he is entering into another phase in his life where he is very involved in setting up a new therapy (PSTEC) to help and assist children in schools throughout the UK; this will eventually become available for worldwide distribution.

Mike is very passionate about his work and shares with you many aspects he has experienced.

Personal Thanks

My inspirations and insights have come from the many people I've met along my journey; without them, I couldn't possibly have written this book. It's been one amazing voyage and I thank you all from the bottom of my heart.

Most of all I would like to thank my wife, Jaqui, for being so understanding and supportive over our thirty-four years together. A thank you to my son Simon, my stepson Steven; my daughters, Helen and Andrea and my beautiful grandchildren and future grandchildren.

Not forgetting my good friend Tim Phizackerley, the owner and creator of PSTEC.

This book is also dedicated to all my teachers and to some very special people who influenced my life's pathway so much in my early spiritual development and gave me so much support as I came to terms with my own personal growth.

Thank you all.

CONTENTS

1. As I Walk With Spirit

At the time of the writing this book I have applied hundreds of past life regressions and hypnotherapy sessions and I have seen many people change for the better after the experience.

Whilst carrying out my hypnotherapy and analytical work I have also been involved in numerous sessions teaching clients how to regress into a past life and helping them to remove a memory cell from their past that may have been interfering with their present life. I have also carried out hundreds of aura readings via my Aura Camera, also linking to people's vibrations and energy and guiding them. Why and for what reason?

Hopefully, my explanation will help you to understand a little more about my work. Remember, this is only my opinion, based on MY experiences over the years, whilst on my spiritual journey. As I continue to learn and walk with spirit, judge for yourself.

This book is not about whether I am right or wrong, it's just my own personal journey and experiences during my life time.

Life on this earthly plane can be very difficult for some people at the moment but I believe the energy is changing rapidly and moving rapidly towards spirituality. People are tired of being lied to and given promises that are never met.

My own personal belief is life will change so much in the next fifty years, spiritually and we will come back to our basic needs. Well, I do hope it does.

Imagine what it would be like to live without the constraints of life or the anxiety connected to it. Well, I believe it will happen when people realise and understand we are surrounded by energy and it's free for us all to use. Our ancestors understood this but it was taken away over the years by greed, wars and politics. Things have to change for us to survive. Money in the future will mean nothing; we will not need it in years to come. We will work together in unity. But, will it happen?

It has to, for us to survive as a race.

2. The Beginning

I was the eldest of six children, born in 1952. My father was a very dominant person and throughout our childhood whatever he said, went without question, or he would be down on us like a ton of bricks. I know because being the eldest, I took the brunt of it all. But that's not really for this book, right now. That's a different chapter in a totally different book. We simply did as we were told. My mother on the other hand was possibly one of the most loving and understanding people you could ever meet. Until her death at the very young age of fifty-seven I never knew her to lose her temper or speak ill of anyone but sadly she died and left us all too soon.

Her favourite saying was: 'If you can't say anything nice about someone then don't say anything and be quiet'. Boy, I should have listened then but I did learn in the end. When you're young you never think of that really.

One of the good things about my childhood and I feel that this has had an influence on my life, is that my parents were not members of a church or particularly religious. Mum believed in God and apparently always said her prayers but was never allowed to mention it to us because my father thought it was poppy cock. Although I was baptised as a Christian, I grew up knowing very little about religion, except of course from the little I learned at school, attending Religious Instruction lessons (which wasn't very often) and a brief period of Sunday school instruction. But I only went because of the free drink of orange juice and sometimes a sandwich.

Even from early childhood I always had a fascination with the mind and how it worked. Although it wasn't until the early eighties I decided to train as a hypnotherapist, joining several institutes in the UK. As I looked back over my childhood, I found it easier as an adult to understand why parts of my personal past lives had linked so much to this present life time. Real or not, judge for yourself; I will go into more detail later.

By way of this book I invite you to follow my own personal journey and to teach you about hypnotherapy and the other fascinating areas of the mind, including energy, healing, imagery, visualisation, chakras, auras, spirit guides and past lives. I will include chapters on Mediumship, Clairvoyance, etc., and my own personal views to each of them.

For many years I have been using an aura video camera and have been astounded by the accuracy in the analysis it gives on a person's aura and energy related areas. Many people have asked me to write about my experiences. So, whilst living in Spain five years ago, I had time to reflect and write. Unfortunately, when I returned to the U.K., my pen drive, holding all that I had written, was mislaid until very recently when it was discovered by my wife. Spirit! Was that you? Maybe I wasn't ready to write this book then but I certainly am now.

3. Hypnosis and Hypnotherapy

The mind has two parts, the conscious part, which you are using whilst reading this book and the subconscious part where everything we feel, see, hear or experience is stored in memory; all our emotions. (This is the computer hard drive.)

First, let's look at what direct suggestion means.

Direct suggestion is where you are relaxed down into hypnosis by the therapist using a calm relaxing voice, with or without soft music playing in the background. The therapist uses his voice and guided imagery to take you into a deep, relaxed state, asking you to imagine certain things and achieve hypnosis. There is no such thing as a hypnotised feeling. It is a state of being where the conscious part of the mind has been slowed down and by-passed making the subconscious more accessible to suggestion.

Through the relaxation process the conscious mind has been slowed down by the use of suggestion and the therapist is able to speak directly to the subconscious part of your mind. You don't have to do anything whilst experiencing this, just enjoy the experience. The therapist guides you and gives you direct positive suggestions pertaining to the problem or issue, reinforcing the subconscious. On completion of the session, you 'awaken', although it is not sleep, this is just a term used by some therapists. On opening your eyes it is normal to feel peaceful and relaxed. You possibly will experience some form of time loss during hypnosis. Some feel they have only been under hypnosis for ten to fifteen minutes, when it has possibly been an hour or sometimes longer. This time loss is normal in hypnosis. I can think of one particular time when a colleague of mine was interrupted during a session and actually locked herself out of her office, with her client still inside under hypnosis. It took her nearly three quarters of an hour to find her landlord, get spare keys and get back into the room. The client was still lying there, quite relaxed, listening to the music. Upon waking, the client was asked how long he thought the session had taken, 'Oh, about twenty minutes', he said.

Direct suggestion therapy can be very beneficial in many areas such as reducing high blood pressure, increasing energy in the ego, helping someone who has trouble sleeping, quitting nail biting, losing weight, examination nerves, driving test nerves; the list is very long.

A good therapist will issue you a CD, similar to the session context, to be listened to at home. The CD is normally a minimum of 30 minutes long and is to be played daily for seven to ten days. This is to programme your subconscious mind through the power of suggestion and repetition. Stage hypnotists use the power of suggestion, the difference being, he or she may want you to quack like a duck when instructed, or do something silly to amuse the audience. Trust me, it works, the hypnotist knows exactly who to choose. They use certain suggestibility tests prior to their actual stage act.

Throughout our lives we all experience the power of suggestion, you just have to look at television advertising and billboards, all suggesting what we should buy. Planting the image into our subconscious, through pictures, words, or sounds, linked to something pleasant. Most of the time, you're not even aware of it. For those of you in the UK do you remember the Bounty Bar, or the Cadbury's Flake advert? I bet right now you are replaying the images in your mind, or singing the song connected to the advert. (Smiles) You brought it back in an instant.

I can remember going to the local cinema when I was very young, and unbeknown to me, (because it happened in an instant), ice-creams and Kiora drinks would flash onto the screen in single frames unseen by the naked eye. Then lo' and behold, when there was a break between films, what would you be craving for? That's right, ice-cream and drinks!

Many years ago, a large store was losing money because of thefts. A trial was carried out whereby a music tape was played in the back ground. Included on the tape were suggestions aimed at the people who stole things, telling them they would feel good about not stealing things today. These suggestions were put onto the tape at a frequency that was only audible to the subconscious part of the mind; you could not hear it consciously. Thefts dropped over night by a considerable amount but because of government legislation it was not and still is not legal to do this. It is called subliminal programming and it is a very effective method when carried out in the correct way.

So let's move on a little bit now and take a brief look at how cause and effect works. I'm not going to get too deep here and I will try to make my explanation as simple as I can.

Every effect must have a cause and its pointless treating the symptom if the cause remains. Let me tell you first how this applies to my therapy.

Imagine that throughout your life you have picked up repressions. A repression is a memory of something that has happened, possibly in your childhood, or as you were growing up and developing which was upsetting to you. It made you feel bad or guilty and at that particular time in your life the energy or emotion linked to it was so powerful your mind repressed it. It's now in your subconscious mind and will protect you from being hurt again. You have no idea of this memory consciously and because it is now firmly embedded within the subconscious part of the mind it has to externalise and identify, in other words, it has to create a symptom to protect you from whatever has happened in the past.

The therapist's job is to guide you back through all those memories to find the repression that is affecting you and help you to remember and release it from your mind. Once the repression is released it can never affect you again. Whatever the symptom or symptoms your mind created to protect you, (or was connected to that memory), will also disappear.

One woman who came to see me, she would be around sixty years of age, and very overweight. During the consultation it became apparent that analytical therapy was right for her. She could not drink coffee, milk, eat bread or fish. She informed me that she was married but she had not been able to conceive and have children.

During the course of therapy, she told me things about her life; but to 'cut a long story short' she had been engaged to a young man who had to go to war but she became pregnant by someone else, an American soldier; she didn't dare tell her family.

One night, whilst alone, she had terrible stomach pains and she lost the foetus down the toilet. She was so frightened that it made her feel sick and she brought up the fish and chips she had eaten that evening. She thought if she had some bread and milk it would help settle her stomach but she brought that up as well. She tried having a drink of coffee but that too came back. This poor young girl was alone and scared, she repressed the whole episode of her miscarriage into the subconscious. She had no conscious memory of the event until it all came pouring out during therapy. She completed and left therapy. Some months later, she contacted me and told me something she had recently experienced. A few months after her therapy she began to experience severe stomach pains and decided to visit her GP, he eventually referred her to a gynaecologist in Harley Street, London.

On examination she was informed that her womb which had always been tilted back was now in the correct position. This had been the reason preventing her from conceiving after her miscarriage. Her subconscious mind had protected her from going through the same terrifying experience again by tilting her womb. She can now enjoy fish, milk, bread and coffee without any reaction what so ever and I remember her laughing saying, 'does this mean I can become pregnant now after all these years'.

This type of therapy is usually spread over a number of weeks, usually up to eight or ten weekly sessions of one hour long. I would expect to see some results by session six or even sooner. Sometimes, though depending how deeply rooted the memory was, a few more sessions might be needed to uncover and release the repression.

Rather than go through all the explanations of cause and effect, I will write a few case histories and let you judge for yourself. Without doubt you will see clearly how and why the mind represses a particular memory and what symptoms could be externalised to protect that person.

Jan and John

Whilst living in Spain in 1984 with my wife and son, we met a couple also from the UK. They owned a small town house in the local village which they used for holidays on a regular basis. We would meet up and go out for the occasional meal; some evenings we would sit outside one of the local bars or by the local pool and have a few glasses of wine.

John was an accomplished artist and produced amazing paintings, very similar to Salvador Dali. All John's paintings were surrealistic. The town house was perfect for John, he had peace and quiet for his commissioned work, and the lighting was perfect for his canvases.

Many evenings would be spent chatting about hypnotherapy and cause and effect and how it could and would affect a person's life.

Jan asked me if I would take her through analytical therapy as she felt she had issues she would like help with. Maybe, it was the discussions we'd had about therapy but something made her become anxious and uneasy. Our talks had triggered something. I agreed to see her the following week at our Villa, for a one-hour evening session; it would be totally private. John and Jaqui would sit on the terrace whilst I worked with Jan inside. It was made very clear from the outset that whatever happened during the sessions Jan was not allowed to discuss it with anyone until therapy was complete. I would also record every session.

One evening, during that week John came knocking on the door, he was in a bit of a panic. It appeared that Jan was in a state and was sitting outside in his car. She was very shaky and had no idea what was happening to her. We quickly got her inside, sat her on the settee and I relaxed her down into hypnosis. She went back into a memory almost immediately. The memory she was reliving was a very unpleasant one. She tried to curl up into the foetal position, began crying and saying, 'leave me alone it's hurting, leave me alone, please don't touch it' as she rolled from side to side on my settee. She was experiencing something from her past with all its intensity and emotion.

Jan was born in Malaysia and was reliving a memory of when she was about four years old and someone was cutting off a protruding part of her umbilical cord or navel. She was trying to shout at the nurse not to touch it; it was sore and stuck to her skin. She was panicking and she was now reliving all of it. After the memory was released from the subconscious she began to settle and calm down.

I spent a little while with her going through certain imagery and visualisation exercises and built up her ego before asking her to open her eyes.

She told me that for as long as she could remember she'd always had a problem with the area around her navel. If anyone tried to go near or touch the area she would get a very nervous, anxious, angry feeling that would last for quite a while. In the memory she told me she could see the scissors and could remember every little detail and the pain she'd felt as they cut her. The anger she felt inside and the intensity of the emotion, she hated the nurse for causing so much pain.

The next day she called to see me and told me that John had touched her navel that morning and she was perfectly fine about it, no more fear, it had gone completely. She also explained that she had never been keen on nurses or hospitals. When the repression had been released, the symptoms left also; cause and effect. I'd not even started therapy with her and things were already beginning to surface

On Jan's first session we did a lot of talking and exploring her childhood to see what other areas may have contributed to certain fears, phobias or present day anxieties. I did a little bit of hypnotherapy for the remaining fifteen minutes of the session, reinforcing her mind to prepare for future sessions.

Jan would go very deep into hypnosis. Some of the memories she experienced through the early sessions of therapy were mainly from her childhood in Malaysia.

Whilst growing up, she had to sleep with her brothers, which led to incest from a very early age. They hurt her terribly and made her bleed. During some of the sessions she would get flash backs of raging water, also a flashback of her uncle's face. Her uncle was a man who she really admired and he featured a lot in her memories during later sessions. To her he was her "knight in shining armour".

Over the next two sessions more came out, more emotion was released. Linked to those memories; anger, guilt, and blame from early childhood.

At about session four, things began to get difficult for her during therapy. She was beginning to get anxious and her breathing was becoming more rapid and shallow. Sometimes her breathing was so fast she couldn't catch her breath and started crying but wasn't able to see anything connected to this emotion. She kicked her legs, as if she was fighting something or someone off. Her arms would move up and down in the chair, imitating a swimming stroke. We were getting really close to the memory and something being released. The session ended at this point and she was extremely uptight.

At the next session, the following week and within a few minutes of being relaxed into hypnosis she went straight into a memory. She was in Malaysia, about seven years old and she was in a tiny homemade flat bottomed boat on a river which was in a severe flood. The river was raging after a very heavy rainfall and she was all alone in this boat panicking how to get back to the bank. Her brother was franticly trying to reach her but she was too far out and the raging current was very strong. She was out of reach of her brother and being swept away by the current. The bank and the edges of the river were high and slimy with mud after a heavy rainfall. She was starting to get frantic in the chair. She kept reaching out and shouting to her brother, 'Help me, help me'. Her breathing was now becoming very fast and shallow, similar to a person hyperventilating. She was very close to passing out.

She leaned over the edge of the make shift boat a little more to reach out for her brother's hand. The boat capsized throwing her back into the river. Panic now set in, this went on for about five minutes with the young child screaming for help as she desperately tried to keep afloat in the raging, swirling river.

She wriggled and squirmed in the chair and at one stage she actually started choking and coughing as she relived going under and swallowing the water. She was very close to drowning and in a frantic desperate struggle to survive the ordeal.

All of a sudden she went very quiet, then she began wriggling again, started shouting 'Pull me up, please, please, please'. Her brother had managed to grab hold of one of her arms but he was having a great deal of difficulty pulling her up the muddy slopes of the river bank. Now, they were both very close to falling back into the river but thankfully her brother managed to grab something and pull his sister to safety.

I recorded every part of this event and over the years I have let many of my students listen to this final part of the session as the repression was released (I had my client's permission for this of course). I've seen students put their hands up to their mouths in disbelief and some have even pulled a jacket over their heads or a lifted a sweater to cover their faces and hide. Jan had no idea, prior to coming into therapy, about any of the river episode or the near drowning experience. What's more, neither did her brother. Everything had been repressed into their subconscious.

I hope you understand now, how a repression works and how it gets pushed deep into the subconscious part of your mind and how it will protect you at all times to prevent that situation ever happening again; possibly by creating fears of things connected to it to keep her safe.

Later that week we met up for a meal and a chat and it was obvious to us that Jan had certainly changed in many ways. The therapy was now complete and she had told John about the things she had experienced during the therapy sessions. Whilst chatting, John told us that Jan hated walking in, or putting her feet into anything that was muddy and would avoid all areas like that to an extreme. I wonder why? Of course it was the mud on the riverbank. Since the release of that memory she has no problem at all with regard to muddy areas or walking through wet sand.

The interesting thing about helping someone release a repression is that once it's been removed or released from the mind, (the subconscious), it has gone and the symptoms that were attached to it have also gone. It can never be viewed the same ever again with the same intensity of emotion. Not every case is as difficult as Jan's. Sometimes what comes out from early childhood development can be so simple, so easily explained as an adult. However, to the child it was so powerful and so overwhelming, the guilt, or anger, or emotion of that experience was strong enough to be repressed into the subconscious. It then externalises as a symptom or symptoms to protect the person in the future. It can externalise in many forms.

Quite a number people have asked me, "How do you know when therapy is complete and there are no more repressions to bring out?" Once it's out and completely removed the client would find it impossible to go back into the repression because it's no longer there and therapy would no longer be possible. I've seen it hundreds of times when I've been checking my work during a later session. The client cannot go back to anything at all and is dismissed from therapy.

My explanation

Imagine that everyone has various repressions within them from early development (which I believe we all do).

During therapy you begin with everyday normal memories, you are then guided back to link and connect with memories which only link to intensity of emotion and intensity of feeling. Once you have linked to one memory it will link to another one and bring it back into the conscious mind for you to see and feel, exactly as it was all those years ago.

In the early part of therapy you are exploring the inside of your own mind, linking one memory to another, especially ones with lots of emotion linked to them. It's a little bit like standing together, (therapist and client) at the top of a hill and making a snowball together. Letting it roll down the hill, gathering speed and momentum, getting bigger and bigger each week, releasing more memories from within the subconscious. Eventually, the snowball cannot get any bigger and bursts open when it gets to the end or bottom of that hill. The repression is released in its entirety and relived through conscious thought. It then dissipates completely and never allows the emotion to return and every symptom connected to it disappears completely.

Every memory is stored in the mind, good or bad and during the therapy you go back into those memories with a feather duster and clean them all out.

Similar to a computer, if there's a problem regarding a virus or corrupt file, you would find it, scan disk, then remove or delete it and conduct a full defragmentation of your computer.

Let me ask this question: When was the last time you defragged your computer; your subconscious mind? (Smiles) Bet you haven't. Well, later I'm going to show you a way of doing this in your own home without the use of hypnosis. It's called PSTEC.

When you're going through analysis, that is exactly what you are doing, cleaning out all the corrupt files and removing anything that is emotionally holding you back. As it has been said, "It's that something inside yourself but outside of your control".

Another thing I would like to make very clear in this book is that you should always consult a doctor before going through any kind of therapy. I make no claim to any form of cure or healing and it's always wise to chat to your doctor first. Always check the therapist's qualifications as most therapists will have letters of recommendation from their clients and display diplomas on the wall certifying their achievements. Also, check that they are fully covered by Public Liability Insurance and have trained with well-known and recognised Institutes. There are many great therapists out there and they can be easily located through a Google search.

Okay, now that's out of the way, let's get on with a few more case histories. The next one turned out to be fascinating and really helped this lady come to terms with something that she'd carried for a long time

Claire

Claire came to see me because she had started having what seemed like panic attacks and very strong feelings of anxiety.

The first session was more talking and finding out when the feelings had started and how long they had been happening. She was a mature student nurse and during her training the panic attacks started. She felt out of place with the young students because of her age but from an early age had always had a passion for nursing. She felt now that her children were older she could train to become a nurse. Even as she was explaining it to me she went into an abreaction. Clearly she needed psychoanalysis to find the root cause of her issues. Direct suggestion therapy may have eased it a little but something in her subconscious was surfacing or creating these issues and needed to be uncovered and released.

The first few sessions released some emotion from her mind and things were going along steadily when during one session she began to have yet another abreaction and panic attack. I tried guiding her to link it to a memory from her past but all she could see was darkness and she felt pressure on her head (I had already realised where she was but as yet, she couldn't see it; she was in the birth canal). She had to see and feel it for herself. A good therapist would never make suggestions, he would let her find this memory herself and would keep guiding her to see the memory clearly and relive it, it would then release all the emotion attached to it.

There were about three weeks of discomfort for her and we couldn't get any further in therapy. She even called me one evening and said that she wasn't coming back for any more sessions but after a lengthy conversation I persuaded her to come for one more session.

The following week she entered my studio looking really tired and extremely anxious. She had not had the best of weeks, not getting much sleep at all, experiencing very vivid and strange dreams. She had stopped going to the teaching school for nurses because of them. She was in a mess mentally and very scared.

I relaxed her down in hypnosis and again she took me back to the darkness and the pressure around her head. She then began to experience a different kind of energy. She could see colours and a white light. At this stage she was panicking, when suddenly she shouted:

'I'm being born, I'm being born. Oh My God, I am being born'!

She told me everything that was happening. The repression was now ready for her to release, her voice was trembling and shaking with fear. I began to ask her questions about what she was seeing and feeling. The first thing she told me was that she could see a woman in blue and next to her was Grandma. At this point she became very angry because she heard Grandma say, 'Oh no, it's a bloody girl, Bob will not be pleased'. She then went on to tell me that at the moment of her birth she couldn't breathe and she was fighting hard to take her first breath but they were so busy with Mum that no-one noticed her struggling. She struggled for a few minutes and it is possible that she went blue before anyone noticed the baby was not breathing properly.

The midwife eventually noticed something was wrong and quickly cleared her airways. Claire felt it all, relived every part of it and quickly started breathing normally.

After I had brought her back out of hypnosis she continued to explain to me what had happened during the memory. Her Mum was bleeding very badly and haemorrhaging and that was the reason the midwife and Grandma were not taking any notice of her. By this time Claire was very relaxed, albeit a little bewildered at what she'd just experienced.

What I hadn't known is that throughout her life she had always had issues with her grandma and very rarely went to see her. She went, as far as to say she hated her but didn't know why. She now understood the reason.

During the week she went to see her grandma and told her all about the therapy and what she had experienced. Grandma sat in total disbelief. Everything Claire had experienced in therapy is exactly what had happened at her birth. Many tears were shared and she and Grandma are now getting on fantastically. She went back to her training, determined to become a nurse and since therapy never experienced another panic attack.

Again, this was cause and effect. The memory of the birth experience is repressed but many people have gone back to it.

I was present at the birth of my daughter Helen and it was one of the most incredible experiences to witness. The birth of a child, especially the birth of your own child is just awesome and very moving.

My first child using Hypnotherapy

Graham

Towards the end of my course to become a qualified Hypnotherapist I had permission to work with certain clients to put my training into practice. We were living in the countryside, in a small hamlet with very few neighbours. I was struggling to find someone close enough to work with until a neighbour told me her son was asthmatic. I explained my therapy to his parents and they agreed to let me try a few sessions with him.

It was made very clear that because of his age, his mother must be present at all times but she wasn't allowed to interfere with the therapy and must remain silent throughout our session. Graham was fourteen years old and had suffered for a long time with chronic asthma.

Their family doctor had been contacted regarding the therapy and told his mother to simply give it try; nothing to lose in any way.

On the first session I relaxed Graham into hypnosis and carried out direct suggestion therapy. In other words I was suggesting to his subconscious mind that he would feel much better and his breathing would become much easier.

Graham's breathing did seem easier for about two days but in real terms it hadn't changed dramatically. I suggested that on the next session we should try to find out when and where the asthma had started and go back more into his memories.

Working with children is absolutely amazing; they go into hypnosis so fast, so deep and so easily. They access memories easily and use really good imagery. Their subconscious mind and memories are very accessible. It's also easier to get deeper-rooted problems from children faster because they haven't had the years or knowledge of adulthood to bury the problems deeper into the subconscious. They haven't developed as many layers.

At the next session I asked Graham, under hypnosis, some very direct questions. The emotions very quickly rose to the surface. The tears started flowing and he was back to a memory at the age of four years old. He was remembering the time he had to go into hospital to have his tonsils removed and the memory he'd repressed was when his mother had to leave him (rejection). He had been so overwhelmed and upset, hardly catching his breath between sobs. He relived the memory with all the emotion and intensity of the feeling that he had experienced at the age of four. It just poured out and poor Mum, now in also tears, sat across from him feeling very guilty. The session ended and I did my best to reassure mum and told her not to feel guilty; she wasn't to blame. Parents at that time were not encouraged to stay in hospital with children. Thank goodness things are different now.

I asked Graham if he fancied jogging down the lane to the farm, about 250 yards. His mum was shocked and said. 'No, he can't'. But he did, twice and never once became out of breath. His asthma never came back; he is now married with children of his own. Where does time go? Wow!

David

When David first called to my home my wife met him at the door and brought him through to my therapy room. My wife had chatted a little to him and had noticed how polite he was and as she put it, "a charming young man".

We chatted for a while and David explained to me what had been happening to him. He was employed as an auctioneer at a local abattoir selling farm animals but recently he was finding it difficult to speak as quickly as he normally would, when selling the animals. This experience was causing him to stutter and his employer had told him he would have to be replaced unless things improved. He was now desperate and didn't want to lose his job.

I told him that we could use hypnosis and divert the stutter into his fingers. At least he would be able to work but it would only be temporary. I also explained to him how finding the cause would help and could remove it completely but he must become completely involved.

Although to find the cause could take many weekly sessions he preferred that direction and his employer had told him if it worked his job would be safe. If it didn't work, he would be looking for other employment. (They didn't mince words back then.)

He was extremely desperate so we began the therapy that evening. David was such a gentle, quietly spoken man and a very sincere person. It was easy to take him into a very deep form of hypnosis and with certain suggestions, carefully phrased, we worked together to find the cause of the problem.

I directed his subconscious mind to link back into the past and to find a very strong emotion which had been formed from his early developing days. It wasn't long before he was recalling a memory from his childhood and with rising emotion he began to cry. I asked what memory he could see and feel. He was very embarrassed to tell me as the tears fell down his cheeks. I left him for a little while before asking him again. He told me that when he was about nine years old he and his brother were trying certain sexual things with each other and he didn't like it. He was very embarrassed to tell me but it was a good start with that one out of the way.

It wasn't long before I had him linking to other memories also connected with the same intensity of emotion and feelings. The session went really well and many of the blocked emotions were released and removed.

On to the third session his mind kept going back to when he was about four years old. He was playing in the orchard at the farm where he grew up. Throughout the session he would get images or memories connecting to the orchard.

He was sat on a swing just enjoying himself in a very relaxed way. The detail he gave was very explicit, all about the crab apple tree that the swing was attached to and the flowerbeds that surrounded the garden, even the smallest details of the perfumes in the garden. He found it very difficult to get away from this memory and remained there for the rest of the session. I felt that something had happened there and the imagery was linked to something connected to the main repression. The one that was making him stammer whilst working.

At this juncture I need to explain that I used a biofeedback monitor (a machine which measures electrical skin resistance); it is attached to the client's hand during the therapy.

Using this machine I could tell immediately if anything was being held back. With David, the needle on the machine had gone off the scale but he couldn't link to anything except the garden and felt perfectly fine enjoying what he was bringing back into conscious thought.

The following week's session began in exactly the same way with him sat in the garden on the swing; but this time he was getting anxious and feeling a little bit nauseated. His thoughts were drawn towards a building opposite the garden and he was feeling very uncomfortable looking at it through his mind's eye.

As often as I tried to get him to go deeper into the memory, the more scared he became; he just couldn't or wouldn't face it. It had surfaced slightly but still it wouldn't release and allow the remaining memory to surface. The subconscious was defending him strongly. I decided to pull away from the therapy and continued the session building his ego and balancing his energy for future sessions by using direct suggestion and putting a number of suggestions into the subconscious. He would be able to go into the memory much faster during the next session and it would be clearer and easier to bring the full memory back. I was preparing him for the following therapy session the best way I could.

David arrived on time as always and wanted to spend some time telling me about how low and tearful he had felt during that past week. I settled him down and took him as quickly as

I could into a very deep state of hypnosis. Again, he went straight back to the memory of the garden but now he saw himself stood in front of the barn looking straight ahead at the large wooden door. He immediately began to feel very scared and the emotion was so strong that his lips were beginning to quiver. He was becoming increasingly anxious and agitated by the second. This was the opportunity as a therapist that I had been waiting for. The transference state was going to allow me to push him further now deeper into those memories. I asked him to open the door and go inside the barn and tell me what he could see. At this point he became very scared and he was wriggling in the chair trying extremely hard and fighting against the memory being released.

Whatever was behind the door and the memory he was about to face would, hopefully, link and connect to the experiences he was having at work. I asked him in a more assertive voice, to open the barn door and go inside and told him that what upset a young developing child's mind would not upset an adult mind, and that it was perfectly okay to go back and remember in detail.

I sat very quietly and watched as he fought against the memory, knowing that I wasn't going to stop the session until the memory was released. It was on the edge and I needed him to push it further.

After what felt like an eternity but was possibly only about thirty-seconds, he began crying. He was telling me in a childlike voice that his dad was killing his pet pig and that he couldn't stop him and he was screaming at him. How his father had pushed him away very harshly. The pig was squealing and sounded as if in much distress. He actually saw his father slit the pig's throat and saw all the blood pouring out. All the emotion that had been attached to the subconscious poured out of David, anger, hatred, guilt and every other emotion linked to that memory.

It wasn't long before David was out of the session and we sat talking, going through his experience and gaining an insight into what had happened that day. Whilst growing up on the farm his father had given him a pet pig to raise as his own pet. Unfortunately, his father hadn't explained that one day it must be slaughtered and the money raised to go into the family kitty. During the rest of his childhood he had many more pets including lambs and a special cow he had received as a birthday present but those pets never left the farm for slaughter, nature taking its course, probably dying from old age.

As you know David worked as an auctioneer and sold farm animals for slaughter or sale. Something had triggered off this childhood memory. It might have been that every time he was selling pigs the subconscious memory of that traumatic day was causing him to stutter preventing the sale of an animal going to slaughter.

Every cause must have a reason (effect) it's a simple fact. The difficulty is getting it to release from the subconscious mind and dissipate through the conscious mind then it has gone forever and can never return; taking all the emotions attached to it.

I didn't really need to see David again but asked him to either call me or write and let me know how he was getting on at work. I did receive a call and everything was as it should be.

He was selling animals, no longer carrying the subconscious guilt, free from his stammer.

I hope these few cases have given you a greater insight into my work using hypnotherapy/psychotherapy and combining cause and effect.

Over the years I've seen hundreds of people and could fill several books on case histories. I am going to share with you how my work has developed from the science of working with the mind in my early days of Hypnotherapy and how the spiritual side of my journey came to be realised.

For a while, after I had qualified as a hypnotherapist I worked at a local Cancer Care Hospice in Lancaster. This was voluntary work and I helped the patients through the trauma of living with Cancer and coping with the side effects of chemotherapy and many other issues. Sometimes I worked with relatives and helped them with the emotions they were experiencing.

I would give relaxation sessions for the staff and nurses before they went home after finishing their long shift.

Sheila's Story

It was whilst I was there that I met Sheila, a woman who'd had one breast removed and the other breast had malignant tumors. She was receiving very intensive treatment. I asked for permission to work with her using psychotherapy, she agreed but only if supervised by a head nurse, as they weren't sure of my work.

Her childhood had been horrendous and for three weeks it poured out of her. After about the eighth weekly session she was feeling much better. The bad memories seemed to have ceased and her mind more balanced. We cancelled the next session of therapy as she was going for another scan.

The following week I received a call from the head nurse, the same one who had sat in and witnessed the therapy. She was very excited and informed me that all the tumors had disappeared completely. I was absolutely delighted with the news and I was called in to see the consultant in charge of the Hospice. He wasn't very happy with me at all and told me I was far to Freudian and he didn't want me back. I was devastated and still to this day cannot understand what his reasons were. I just wonder if he felt threatened in some way by my work and was a teeny bit jealous. Maybe "HE" should have had a few sessions in my chair.

Sheila, the woman I had worked with, sent me a lovely poem and a very personal, handmade card, which I will treasure always. The best news, however, was that her Cancer had gone into full remission. Was it the Chemo or was it my therapy? It doesn't matter in the slightest.

Sheila's' poem:

Facing the unknown sitting in a comfortable chair
A voice inside me says, "BEWARE"
These negative feelings, fears about myself, I have stored,
Locked away so long in a corner of my mind,
Will be brought out and relived, the pain and shame
All the hostility when I took the blame
Each hurt and anger from the past
Now comes to life again, but now it is seen at last
As something that worried a childish mind
Cannot hurt an adult's, I will find
But the frustration I feel over the weeks of treatment leaves no doubt
That the things in life I never cared about
Now take on a new significance they seldom did before,
Although the pain of reliving scenes of childish terror and woe
When all I feel is hate and want to run away and go from that dreaded chair and probing voice. Yet I return each week; Even though pain tears me apart
And I wonder how much therapy I can take from the start
When now at last there is a break from pain;
I am a new person and can cope again
Whilst this Curative Hypnosis gives me hope
As the therapist in his wonderful way
Helps me see that whatever troubled me deep in my mind before
Is out in the open at last, it has gone, I need never feel guilty anymore,
I can begin to enjoy each brand new day as it brings
Something special to see in simple everyday things;
Because this radical approach to my problems will
Help me feel positive about myself as a person
The negative feelings inside my head
Now have disappeared, and a confident person emerged instead.

God Bless you Sheila. What you had written for me is so moving, and I thank you from the bottom of my heart for sharing this poem.

4. Past Life Regressions

To explain more about this fascinating subject I'm going to give you a little background about myself as a child, growing up. Hopefully, later, you will be able to understand how my life in the present is so linked to my own past life. Well, maybe, but who really knows.

As a child from about the age of nine years old my mother would never know where I was, I just loved being out in the countryside and enjoyed playing in the nearby fields where we lived. I also used it as an escape from certain areas of my abusive childhood.

I lived on the edge of a very large council estate with open country behind our rear garden. From an early age I remember playing with friends, playing 'Cowboys and Indians' (typical kid's stuff). Of course, at that time, I did not know why but I would never be or pretend to be anything other than an Indian. Not many of my friends wanted to be an Indian they always wanted to be the cowboy, of course that meant I was the one always being pursued and chased. Even then, no matter how hard anyone tried to make me change my mind, the more determined I would become and remain a Native Indian.

Christmas was always a new Native Indian outfit. I eventually grew up and let go of the passion I had held so dear to me as a young child. Well, that's what I thought. As I got older I became fascinated watching movies of Cowboys and Indians.

It became more of a passion and I was reading more about the culture of Native Americans.

I was about the age of eleven and had started secondary school but I used to get into so much trouble for playing truant. I dread now, thinking back, just how many days I actually did truant from school (hangs head in shame).

My poor mother was always speaking to the school making excuses for me. It wasn't that I didn't like school because I did and that's the strange thing. I was in the A forms all through my schooling and achieved very good grades; but I preferred being out in the countryside or woodlands of the Lake District where I grew up. I always craved the outdoors and the freedom of the open countryside or exploring new pinewoods or hardwood areas. It was my passion. Okay, I hear you saying, 'many children would love to do that', but wait until you hear my past life, then you can put your own thoughts to it.

At the age of twenty-one I married and within the first three years I had become the proud father of two beautiful and fantastic daughters. My life was plodding merrily on its lovely pathway, without a care in the world, working as a stone mason which was my main income and taxidermy during the winter months.

During that time I was developing a fascination for Wolves. I just thought that they were amazing animals, especially the white ones. I was starting to take an interest again in Native American culture, native music, artifacts etc..., in fact, to this day, I love listening to my native music.

So what has this to do with Past Lives? Be patient because we are getting there slowly.

Okay, let's look and think about what a past life is. You don't have to believe in it but for the moment all I ask is that you open your mind and read about what others have experienced. Where does it come from? How do we remember it so clearly after experiencing a past life regression? Why it is there and what purpose will it have now, in this life? All will be revealed. Well, hopefully.

Imagine that you may have had many previous lives and in those previous lives, you possibly had a theme to follow, a life's plan.

What would have happened if that life suddenly ended without you fulfilling that plan?

This is what's called a Cell Memory and it could possibly be brought forward from that past life into this present life. The cell memory is now in the subconscious mind of your present life, like a form of spiritual DNA hidden behind the scenes.

This was my own Past Life experience

It was in the early 80's, my wife, Jaqui and I saw an advert in one of our local papers advertising Hypnotherapy/Past Lives.... Well, that was enough for me, my eyes lit up and suddenly I was on the phone and had booked an appointment within minutes. I literally had no idea what it was about or what I was doing, but something inside my mind made me very curious. It was like I was being drawn but of course I didn't know why.

The studio was in Kendal, I met a really pleasant female therapist. She explained to me in detail what could possibly happen. She sat me in a chair, in a reclined position and placed a cover over me. She talked to me for about ten minutes, asking if I'd ever experienced a past life before and explained what might happen, she also said, nothing may happen. By this time, I was getting a little anxious.

In the background, relaxing music was playing and the lady with her calming voice guided me into a really deep relaxed state of hypnosis. She then suggested that I could see a tunnel, like a tunnel of peace and that I was lying down in a boat, allowing myself to drift into the tunnel and allowing myself to drift back in time. She kept repeating, 'all the way back', 'and all the way back'. I could see and feel myself drifting into this calming tunnel but I certainly didn't feel I was going back in time.

I remember thinking; I don't think this is working, although I felt very, very, relaxed.

After what felt like ten minutes she asked me to imagine the tunnel opening wider and see myself drifting into the side to stop the boat. I could see this clearly in my mind. I was then asked to describe what I could see. Suddenly, my heart started racing I could see the most magnificent range of distant snow and ice covered mountains. I was asked to look down and see what I was wearing and describe what I could see. I started laughing and told her I was wearing some kind of suede outfit, it was also across my midriff, with tassels flowing in the breeze. I also had on some type of leggings.

I was asked if there was any water or a lake near to where I was standing and within seconds I was looking at my reflection.

In that reflection stood a tall, slim, young man with a deeply tanned skin; long black hair fastened back into a ponytail, with a single white feather in the left side of his hair. I was asked my name and my reply was immediate. My name is John Satchel and my father's name was also John but he's dead now. At this point in the past life I had become part of it and was living it in every detail. I was asked by the therapist to take her through everything that was happening and to tell her all about my family, where I lived and the year. Again my replies were immediate.

It was 1852 and the country was North West Alaska. My father is dead but my mother's name is Neonah and I have a brother called Simon and it's for me to look after both of them. (Wonder if that is why my son in this life was named Simon) never thought of that before, anyway let's move on.

I started by explaining that my father had come from England and whilst trapping, became very friendly with the Indians, taking them food and skins and trading with them. He fell in love with Neonah and lived with her for many years. I was the first born, followed by my brother Simon many years later. We lived in a log cabin which overlooked a small lake. My father built this for us. Unfortunately he died of a bronchial illness which left me to look after my mother and brother.

Everything was so vivid – just over the ridge was a small native village of about fifteen tepees and I was asked to describe it all in great detail.

I could describe everything, the clothes, the countryside and the people, even down to the name of my elder (grandfather) whose name was Nahkoma. I could recall every little bit of detail; suddenly I was asked if I had a girlfriend. Immediately stood right next to me was Jeanne. It was as if time had moved forward, just a little. She was tall, slim and was wearing a slightly off white cotton type dress but nothing like anything I had ever seen before. All I could feel was how much in love with her I was. It was then I knew where the white feather had come from, Jeanne had given it to me. She also had one in her hair; it was from the Sea Eagle.

Jeanne used to help me with my mother and my brother, Simon. My mother would sit on the porch of the cabin and gently rock forwards and backwards; just sitting there, with a type of clay pipe in her mouth; all the time just staring into space, hardly ever speaking. I knew she was missing my father desperately and had no further wish to continue her life without him.

Jeanne had rescued and reared a female white wolf pup which had been abandoned at about the age of eight weeks old. She had named the pup, Tewka and you would never see Jeanne without Tewka walking beside her. Everything about the past life I was experiencing was of peace and love, involving family bonds and how balanced and peaceful life was there.

My therapist then asked me to drift forward in time to the next important part of my life. I began to feel very upset. I started to fill up with emotion. What happened next was devastating. Tears were streaming down my face and I couldn't speak.

My therapist guided me into the memory and with my voice quivering and tears streaming down my face I struggled to tell her because of the power of the emotion. Men on horses had charged into the village and were killing innocent people. Women and children were being shot or slashed with swords, indiscriminately. Dust flew everywhere and as it started to clear I could see Jeanne lying face down on the floor with blood all over her back. Tewka, laid by her side, also covered in blood. This part of my past life seemed to go in slow motion. I ran to be with Jeanne and held her in my arms, blood trickling from the corners of her mouth, she was dead. The feeling of pain was tremendous, almost unbearable, reliving the murder of my family, the people closest to me, dead. Tewka survived her injuries, I nursed her back to health and she walked with me, by my side, for the rest of her life.

I was then asked to go forward in time to the next important part of my life; all I could see was the inside of a tepee and I was laid on my back looking up. I was asked what was happening; I replied, “I think I'm ready to leave this life, I'm so tired”. I was about 80 years old and had spent the remainder of my life with my mother's people and the few who had been spared. They were standing around my bed, many of them crying; along with my brother Simon. I felt that I had taken the place of my Grandfather and became a teacher to many over the years and was an extremely well respected elder of the village.

I was asked to let go and everything would be fine. It was then that the most amazing thing happened. As I let go, I actually felt my soul leave my body and I could look down and see everyone. I had the most unconditional feeling of love inside me. Words cannot describe what I felt. I wasn't a body, I was energy. Then, all of a sudden, Jeanne was there with my mother and father. Grandfather and Tewka were also there, I could feel and see them so clearly. It was all seen and felt as pure energy not bodies.

My therapist let me stay with them for a little while and after about five minutes she told me she was bringing me back to this life. She asked me to think of where I lived, and what year it was. Where I had been and who I had been with. Within ten-seconds I was back. I think my first words as I opened my eyes were, WOW!

I was sat in that chair thinking this is something I'd like others to feel and experience. I want to teach this. That afternoon changed my life's direction completely.

I began training soon after, and became a professional Hypnotherapist within a few years and as they say 'the rest is history'.

Now can you see how my past life came through into this life? Remember the early part of my childhood. Hopefully, you will now understand a little more about cell memories and how they may carry forward into the present life.

Since that first past life I've been back hundreds of times, exploring events deeper in my mind and I am now in the process of writing another book all about Tewka; based on my past life experiences. Tewka was the white wolf from my past life and when I write, I become Tewka and see through her eyes and write about her life and experiences. It's great fun writing this story.

In my early days of guiding people into past lives I used to record the sessions and give the cassettes to the client; or students who were studying past lives for further exploration and clarification, (with the client's permission, of course). Sometimes the results after research, were so astoundingly accurate.

I was more scientific in those early days (and may have been possibly a little unsure) as I would spend a considerable amount of time getting as much detail as I could from the person to establish the accuracy of the past life details. Things such as: names, dates, years, and details of what they could see, or in which country they lived. Clothing, dates on newspapers or documents, details that could verify the authenticity. Sometimes, there was no traceable evidence and many scientists believe it's the mind playing tricks or a "wish fulfillment". Over the years I learned that I did not need proof but could use the information to help in my healing work. If a cell memory has been brought forward from the past to this present life, for whatever reason, and it's affecting a person's quality of life, I helped to find it, remove it and the client would have a better quality of life in the future. Once the memory has been brought forward from the past into the present and released it will never again have a negative effect in this life.

The next case history will give further insight into cell memory and just how it can affect people and relationships. The personal names of each case history are of course changed to protect the client's identity, unless I have their sole permission to name them.

Steve and June

Whilst I was in practice as a Hypnotherapist I met a young couple who came to see me regarding a problem they were both experiencing.

During their initial interview they told me that they had been together for over six years but had been married for only three months. Prior to getting married they had both agreed on no sex before marriage.

They were a really charming couple and it was obvious they were very much in love but were experiencing difficulties when it came to the bedroom department, (sex). I explained to them that I wasn't a sexual therapist and maybe they should go elsewhere but after a thirty-minute chat they said they preferred to try hypnosis. I did make it very clear that we should be looking deeper and finding out what the cause was.

Steve was adamant he wanted them to try hypnosis, his wife agreed so I made them an appointment; two, one-hour sessions in a week's time.

After only a couple of sessions it was obvious that the direct suggestion therapy just simply wasn't going to help. In fact, it seemed to be getting worse, not better. I told them I would try one more session the following week. There would be no charge and if it didn't work I would make them an appointment to see a different kind of therapist.

I drew on all my knowledge but I was struggling. I was at a loss and had really no idea what to do with either of them. My only hope was that they would both agree to try analytical therapy. They arrived on time as always, Steve came in first, I looked at him and smiled but could tell he was down and completely fed up.

To this day I don't know what made me ask him but I just came right out with, "Hey do you fancy trying a Past Life tonight?" He looked at me with a curious sort of grin and said he wasn't sure that he believed in past lives but he'd be willing to try anything at that moment.

Well it was my suggestion so I began to ease Steve into a past life. By now he was so used to relaxing it was easy to get him into a very deep state of hypnosis and with some guided imagery I guided him back into a past life. In the past life he had a sister who was also called June, he described her in detail and they were extremely close. He told me the family lived in Canada and he gave me the names of his parents, aunts, uncles, and the year and described where he lived; everything in amazing detail. The session continued for about an hour and at the end I asked him to open his eyes and be back with me in the Centre.

As he opened his eyes he said, "That was amazing, it's no wonder I can't touch my wife, she was my sister in a past life". Wow, and he started smiling; it had been quite a while since I'd seen him this happy.

He began telling me more about the past life, everything he had seen and experienced. He said, "It makes so much sense now".

I was sat there listening to all he said but I wasn't sure exactly what had just happened. Was this a way of his mind making an excuse, or was it a wish created by his subconscious to by-pass the critical factor?

Steve went into the other room; there was no possibility of June knowing what had just taken place. I called her through and told her that Steve had tried a past life and asked if she would she be willing to try one. She agreed, although, naturally quite nervous.

Once the past life was established I simply asked her where she was and to my complete surprise she said Canada. I also asked her if she had any family (you ahead of me yet?). What happened next nearly made me fall out of my chair. She very quietly, in almost a whisper said, 'I've a brother called Stephen'. Suddenly she sat bolt upright, making me jump with her, saying in a very loud voice, 'Oh my, Oh my'. She had returned to the present day really fast, she had pulled out of the past life so fast she was shaking all over.

It didn't take long for her to balance out and I called Steve through to join his wife. I made them both a cup of tea and let them talk through what had just happened. Could this be real? Could it be that their past life had affected them in this present life? Of course it may have done. As a therapist, I was to be left totally dumbfounded by this result.

Later that week I received a lovely letter from them, it said everything was and had become 'normal' now and they thanked me for all my help. Well of course, it wasn't me, it was their past lives. Wasn't it? A double cell memory. I've only seen it this once in my work so far but you never know I may see it again. (Smiles)

In past a life, you may have been someone's sister and in this life you're their mother. I've seen this many times, fathers and sons changing places. So be warned, be very careful about the mother-in law jokes! One never knows, does one?

Sometimes I had evening appointments at home, as not everyone could come and see me through the day. Two women came together, (Rose and Susan) one was for weight loss and the other for confidence. They both just wanted a few sessions to help them out. Rose asked me one night if she and Susan could experience a past life because they both believed in them and they had seen my brochure advertising this type of therapy.

Susan

First to go was Susan, a small, stocky woman who was troubled with her breathing. She told me that she had suffered since she was very young and over the years it hadn't improved. Her charisma was just amazing, she was always jolly, fun to be with and such a lovely, lively person.

She relaxed into hypnosis and went back to the early 1800s in Holland. She described everything about her dress and her home and before I had chance to ask her any more questions she began to get very anxious and started breathing very heavily. She was now finding it extremely hard to catch her breath and found it very difficult to speak, "So much smoke, so much smoke, I can't breathe, I can't breathe" she kept saying in a frantic manner. She was waving her arms about in the air.

She then told me that there had been a fight in the village with a rival gang and her house had been set on fire. She was hiding in the cellar with her arms around her two daughters, protecting them. They were screaming and crying uncontrollably. She was holding the lining of her dress across the children's mouths to help them breathe. The room was filling up with smoke and it was obvious that she and her children were going to die. At this point she went really quiet and her breathing slowed down, I asked what was happening and Susan said, "Everything's fine now, we're floating and safe, it's peaceful, here".

I asked her if she had died and she replied, "Oh Yes, we all died". She had now entered into the shining level of energy. I had experienced this shining level in my own past life and the feeling experienced cannot be put into words.

When I brought her back to the present time and she'd had time to dry her eyes with the tissues I always keep close at hand, I noticed something. Susan's breathing was much easier now and her chest seemed much more relaxed. I asked her how she felt and she told me she felt fine but was quite understandably unsure about what had just happened to her.

Apparently, unbeknown to me, in this life she had always had a fear of flames and smoke and didn't like anything to do with straw. In her past life the roof of the house, the one that had been burning had been made of straw.

It all linked the cell memory of the past with her present life she had difficulty with her breathing, her life ending all too soon. It had been released and I was curious to know if those fears still remained.

Since her past life, her breathing is now fine and all her fears regarding smoke, flames and straw have disappeared.

Rose

One of the first things I noticed about Rose was her lack of confidence. Whilst chatting to her she told me that as far back as she could remember she had always felt this way. I didn't know her age but guessed she was in her mid-sixties. One interesting thing about Rose, she had always been cold and was so fed up with the doctors not being able to give her a reason why she always felt that way. She'd had scans, blood tests and taken various medications but nothing had helped. When I touched her hand, her skin was really ice cold.

Once her past life had been established, Rose began to show lots of emotion. She was a little girl in the back streets of Liverpool, about the age of five and the year was 1763; the month was January. She was very upset because she couldn't find her mother; tears were streaming down her face. She laid down huddled up behind an old run down building. Rats were running around the area and she told me the place smelt really bad, as did she.

I asked her to describe to me what she was wearing and where she was. She was wearing a thin tatty old dress, no shoes or socks and it was the middle of winter, she was so cold she felt that she was freezing to death and just wanted her mum. The past life was so emotional for her, it quickly went quiet. She went forward into the shining level and let go of her cold, little body from that life.

Soon, she was smiling and telling me that her mother had come to meet her and now she was happy. I asked her to describe where she was and her face lit up as she told in a childlike voice 'this feels like heaven, and my mummy is here with me now'.

After the session was over we chatted more about what she remembered from her past life. She suddenly told me she was feeling warm, and said, "It's all because of that past life isn't it? I just smiled. Of course I didn't know the answer. I saw her the following week just to see how things had gone since the past life. She came into the studio beaming, what a different person. She was all smiles, chatty and had good eye contact. Without doubt there was a great change in her, not just in her, but in her appearance also.

She told me that night after her session, when she went to bed; she had deliberately gone back into the past life and now knew what had happened in Liverpool, on that fateful evening. Her mother had been a prostitute and had been killed by two drunks. No one knew about Rosie, so didn't realise she was missing. Slowly she died, cold and alone in a dark, and dirty back street. Since the session, Rose said she had felt warm and had much more energy. It certainly had changed her in many ways, even her children couldn't believe the difference in her attitude and the confident way she now approached things. Just before leaving my studio…. She said “Oh, by the way, I’d always hated rats but not anymore”, and she left, laughing.

Roger the Leg

Roger had booked a past life some three weeks prior, he was a large man and came into my studio on crutches.

I settled him as comfortably as possible. He’d never experienced hypnosis before so I explained what would happen. Somehow, we deviated and he began to tell me about his right leg. He explained that for over thirty years he’d had a problem but no one seemed to be able to sort it out for him. The top thigh muscle was wasting away, very slowly and he was in great discomfort but that wasn't the reason he had come to see me. He had seen one of my local adverts regarding past life regressions and said he felt as if he was being drawn to come and experience it for himself.

It wasn't long before he was in a past life and his first words were: “Oh dear, the noise here is deafening”. He was a male aged about 26 and was wearing a uniform. He was in the middle of a battlefield in France during a civil war. He described the carnage, the smell of blood, and the rotting corpses of the dead and dying. There were hundreds of soldiers and horses, laying there in their own blood, shot, parts missing. He shuddered and said he wasn't comfortable about what he was seeing. He could smell gunpowder and hear the screaming of people in pain. It was then he shouted, “I’VE BEEN HIT, I’VE BEEN HIT”. He felt a thud and got a burning sensation in the thigh of his right leg, the bullet had hit an artery and blood was pumping out of it. He started to tremble in my chair, and was getting very upset, so I gently guided him and brought him back to the present day. He had gone to the cell memory straight away and I knew it would be okay for him to return safely.

He opened his eyes and took a deep breath and said, “Phew”. He asked if he could get a drink of water, as he felt thirsty and a bit dehydrated. He got out of the chair and walked over to my sink, filled a glass with water. He took a long drink and walked back, looking at me in a puzzled way, possibly still wondering what had just happened. At this point he hadn't realised that he was walking without his crutches, and without any sign of a limp or pain. He said, “That was so real, wow, I felt the bullet hit my leg and I could see all the blood spurting out, I knew I was going to die”.

He went into more detail of what he had seen and felt. He was completely stunned and sat in the chair, in disbelief. I brought to his attention that he’d walked, unaided, to get himself a drink. The pain and the limp had gone.

I was as amazed as he was and for some reason I asked him…. “Have you got a birth mark anywhere on your body”. He looked at me and pointed to his right thigh and said, “Oh, My God, here; right where the bullet went in”. This was a classic example of a cell memory being brought forward into this present life.

I often wonder what a doctor or surgeon would think, maybe that we had all lost the plot but now I was obtaining what looked like more proof. I no longer even try to explain it. All I know is it worked for him and surprise, surprise, his leg healed. Oh, I forgot to mention, he spoke fluent French and wouldn't go anywhere else for his holidays except France. He said he was going to do some research and I do hope he found the answers he was searching for. I've a very strong feeling that he would have.

During my own development into past life regressions I was very fortunate to experience many people's past lives.

Okay, let's hold our thoughts and change direction for a little while. I want to take you back to something that happened when I had finished my training in hypnotherapy.

The teacher always told us that if we were going to take people through analysis, then we should experience analysis ourselves and take a dose of our own medicine. I had a colleague who lived quite close to me. He and I had studied and finished the course at the same time. He agreed to take me through analysis one Saturday afternoon.

Well, it was a change for me, being sat in his chair. I relaxed very well and soon things poured out. Lots of nasty childhood memories and emotion, it all just came flooding out. At one stage I was spinning in the chair feeling very sick and every time I tried to stop it, it got worse. Poor John was stunned. He had never experienced anything like this before and had to stop the session. We had run over time and he had another client in the waiting room. I sat in another room with a cup of tea and couldn't stop shaking. I think I spilled more than I actual drank. John returned at the end of his client's session and said: "What the hell was that?" I had calmed down by this time but could only reply, "I've no idea". Neither of us had a clue about what had just happened or what it meant.

Let's leave that there and return to my other past life...

Years came and went but even as an adult I was still doing this silly thing of lining up any mark on my car windscreen and using it like a site of a gun, but I had no idea why. Maybe it was to break the boredom of long journeys.

One evening whilst I was working at my computer, sitting listening to someone talking about Tarot cards, my mind started spinning and I began to feel quite sick. I closed my eyes. I was spinning and spinning and then I could see land, way, way beneath me as if I was up in the clouds. I was in a Spitfire and I was engaged in an air combat between the English and Germans. My plane had been shot at and I had been hit in my side with a piercing bullet. I could smell and taste the smoke that was filling my cockpit and lungs and I was slowly dying. I could feel life leaving me, I was spinning and spinning and plummeting to earth. I know I died before I hit the ground because the last memory I had was looking at my screen and then all went quiet and dark. I opened my eyes and could not believe that over an hour had elapsed.

I remembered everything, memories just clicked into place, as I sat up smiling. In that life my name was David. I was only 18 years old and I was shot down over the English Channel fighting for my country. That cell memory had been present in my session with John but neither of us understood why, how could we? It was exactly the same spinning sensation. We were both very inexperienced at that time. To this day, if I ever go and watch any air displays, it's always the Spitfire I love to watch. As a young child I was keen to join the R.A F. but never did because other things prevented me from doing so. But my son Simon joined at the age of eighteen and he loves it. Strange how things in life can sometimes reverse themselves, or maybe it was just good old parental guidance.

It's amazing how many past lives link to the present life and just recently some of the well-known television presenters and famous Hollywood film stars have shared their experiences on live television. Even the sceptics are somewhat baffled with the accuracy of some past lives. But as I've always said, you judge for yourself. Sometimes there isn't an explanation and if there was, well, maybe we would be sat in heaven, wherever or whatever your heaven is. Even after all these years I am still amazed when working with energy how simple it can be to help a person to balance their energy. I am still amazed how it can bring about a life change in them for the better. The human mind is such a powerful tool when it is used properly and we as therapists have so much more to learn and understand.

Many people have asked me if it is dangerous going into a past life, well during all the years I have been practicing I have never seen or heard of anyone dying or having any permanent damage. In fact, it's usually quite the opposite, even if the past life is very emotional it seems to have some sort of clearance effect.

Most people just open their eyes after the session and smile. Many have telephoned or written to me, often a few weeks later, to let me know that certain things in this life, things that had been bothering them and had been linked to their past life experience have now gone. Strange or not, real or not, it has worked so well for so many people.

Oh, and by the way, I've still not had Cleopatra or Mark Anthony yet but I certainly have had a good many Egyptian past lives; some in places of high power but some just everyday ordinary people but all with so much detail. Many of my clients have experienced Native American lives. In fact, there have been so many different past lives it would take me forever to write about them.

If you would like to experience a past life I suggest you find a qualified therapist, one who has been established for a number of years and has expertise in this area. If you have had a past life experience which changed your life and would like to share your experience, then please email me at **www.mwhypno@yahoo.co.uk**. I cannot guarantee to reply to you all but I will certainly do my best, or you could visit my website at (**www.mwhypno.co.uk**) and email me via the web link'

Is every past life emotional? No, it is not and I've had witnessed many past lives that have been wonderful and very enjoyable to listen to. But as normal I try to get as much information as possible from that past life. Dates, names, types of dress, places, etc. Many people ask if you remember your past life once you're brought out of hypnosis. The answer is that you remember every single detail and you can explore it further any time you wish by relaxing yourself down and bringing the past life back into your thoughts. I suggest that you do it before going to sleep. I've been back into many of my past lives over time.

Over the years, I have made many friends on the internet and Jackie and her husband Alan are just two of them. Jackie had an interest in past lives and came to see me whilst taking a weekend break. Here she tells her story in her own words and what she experienced.

My Personal; Past Life Experience - By Jackie

Hi there! Most of you might think, "But how do I find a therapist who specialises in past life regression?" Well, the therapist who helped me experience my past life regression was a person called Mike Wells who lives in Morecambe in the UK

I have always been interested in past lives but knew nothing about the subject and I certainly had not experienced a past life regression before I met Mike in his room on Pal talk. The subject fascinated me, so the end of February 2005, I decided to spend the weekend in Morecambe and meet Mike, Jaqui and his family to discuss past life regressions in more detail.

After talking with Mike at his home, I asked him if he would, try to do a past life regression session with me, and so it began.

As I suffer from a bad neck due to a car crash years ago, we thought it might be best if I lay down for the session. It is usually done sitting relaxed in a chair. It began with Mike telling me to focus my eyes on a certain spot on the ceiling of the room and slowly he counted down with numbers, my eyes began to feel so heavy, I had to close my eyes, I could hear him talking to me. I began to feel more and more relaxed, and in my mind I could see a beautiful colour of light purple surrounding me. Oh, it felt so peaceful and then I seemed to see flowers all around me, all colours, they looked so wonderful. As I tried to look past the flowers I noticed a young woman, she was so beautiful, and she was wearing the flowers I had seen in her hair. Mike asked, "Who is she?", and I answered, "She is my sister, and she is getting married soon." I could see myself as a little girl, oh I was so proud of her, and my parents were there, Mary and Henry. Not sure of the year, but it seemed the clothes we were wearing must have been maybe 200 years old, if not more. Then I saw my sister, older. She seemed in her thirties, and she was in bed. I was sat next to her crying, because she was dying. I could see myself, heavily pregnant, but later had lost my baby girl due to the upset (In my present life I cannot carry girls, I miscarry, but I have 2 sons).

Then, I just seem to see the beautiful light purple light again; it seemed to swirl round me, like I was going through a tunnel. I saw a wounded man, he was badly injured, and he was laying on some sort of bed made from logs and twigs on the floor, I heard Mike's voice say, "Is this you?" and I seem to shout with so much emotion, "NO this is not me, it's my friend David", but I pronounced it DAV_ ID. "He is a traitor to the royal family, and I can't help him, I want to, but it's too late, he is dying". I repeated "He is a traitor, and he stole the box, and I can't take it back because they will know who did it, and he was my friend, he used to wear the armour, I wear". I looked down at myself, and saw I was wearing a suit of armour. I heard Mike's voice again asking, "Where are you?" And I shouted at him, it's "Dover! I see the castle on the hillside, wow, it's so big, seems to stretch so long with all the buildings". I said, "I must hide the box now, they can't find out that he took it, and I want my friend to die without everyone knowing that he was a traitor".

(The funny thing is in this life, I hate traitors, and I seem to use the word when someone is bad.)

I kept saying, "The tree which stands alone on the hillside, near the castle, I feel I buried it there".

The box wasn't quite square, longer width than depth with fancy designs on the corners of it, but I know what is inside it, It must not be found by the wrong hands, as it's very important. I then return to the beautiful purple light again, and Mike asked me to begin to open my eyes. I opened my eyes slowly, I felt so relaxed as I woke, but what seemed like five minutes was actually well over an hour. As I sat up I got a bursting sensation and I turned to Mike and said, "Oh, sorry but I must use your toilet". I returned to talk to Mike and said, "I am sorry, I was bursting and couldn't stop". He smiled at me and said, "That's okay, it's natural, it's like a cleansing". As Mike and I were talking he said to his wife Jaqui, "I wonder if there is still a castle in Dover today". None of us knew, so he turned on his pc and searched for Dover Castle. Up came a picture and to my surprise, wow! I was in shock, there in front of me was the long castle stretching across a hillside just how I saw it and I am sure you can guess what we looked for next, yes! The single tree near to the castle on hillside, and there it was! You can imagine my shock! So there we were, all thinking: "Do we drive down to Dover with a shovel?" Well, I am sure you can imagine we wanted to, but as Dover is about six hours drive away we passed on that one for now! But hey you never know what the future holds? Anyway, if you ever hear of a women getting arrested for digging under a tree in the grounds of Dover castle, "It just might be me!" She said.

EGYPT

Because of my link with my guide, Joshua, I always was and I'm still very drawn to Egypt and its culture. My wife and I are looking forward to the day when we will be able to go and spend a few weeks exploring the Pyramids, go to the Valley of the Kings and the many other interesting places. It's something we have wanted to do for many years and I do hope before my time is over I will be able to go and see it all. For some reason, it will be like going home and could be quite emotional. But let's wait and see.

This brings me to another past life I experienced but as yet, not much to remember as I've not yet gone into it in more detail. I was in Egypt, a small boy, aged about five years old. My father was a carver of stone and we lived very close to where he worked. We lived amongst many hundreds of other workers and families but everyone was poor and worked long hours for very little food. My father made me steal things for us to survive but it was something I hated doing. I haven't made much more progress on this past life but in this life I cannot tolerate anyone who steals, (in that life, as I said, my father was a stone carver) and in this life I have been a stonemason for many years. "Hmmm makes you think a bit."

I hope this has given you an insight into my work on past lives and for me it has been a fascinating journey. Do I know if it is real? I will leave that up to you to fathom out because I simply do not know the answer. I know what my own feelings are and I will continue with past lives.

5. Aura Cameras and Auras

Quite a few years ago, as it was getting close to Christmas, I was sat at my computer chatting to a woman from Australia; via my Chat room on the internet. She was talking about a camera that could display images of a person's Aura and take a photograph. Wow! I thought.

At that time of the year work was slow and irregular and bills still to pay. There were Christmas presents and food to buy but there I was looking at and thinking of purchasing an Aura camera at a cost of over $6,000 dollars. My wife thought that I had lost the plot completely but within a few days I had arranged a loan through my 'friendly bank manager'. (Smiles) What an investment, I hadn't a clue how it worked, I just knew it would become part of my work, don't ask me how I knew, because I really didn't have a clue. (We can always blame Josh my guide).

It arrived a few weeks later, I remember the day well. I received a phone call telling me I had to pay customs import duties of over £400 Sterling before the camera could be released. (Ouch! I didn't expect that.) They forgot to tell me about import duties. Christmas just became a lot more expensive!

I was like a kid with a new toy and couldn't wait to get going. I loaded the program into my laptop, connected and just couldn't wait to see my aura on screen. What would it look like? I sat there spellbound as the biosensor picked up on the energy around my head and shoulders and projected it onto the screen. I had never seen anything like it, I was totally amazed and mesmerised; a live video of my own energy or aura. I hadn't a clue what I was looking at or what the colours meant. My heart raced with excitement.

Once the sensor was calibrated and after taking a head shot of my own Aura I froze the programme and began to print the twenty-two-page analysis. As it was printing I went through the rest of the programme, not really knowing what I was looking at. I was absolutely amazed by the amount of information given and shown on screen. As my thoughts changed, so did the colours of the aura energy as did the energy in my chakras. They altered as my thoughts altered. It was one amazing experience.

With the package came lots of reading and full explanation via CD's and paperback books on how to use the aura video station. It wasn't long before I was totally engrossed, learning about chakras and auras. My own printout was amazingly accurate, as was my wife's. Friends and family were also astounded at the accuracy. I just couldn't get Max, my Springer Spaniel to keep his pad on the sensor long enough. Ha! Ha! I did try, honest but I don't think he was too pleased with me. Well, he must have an aura; after-all, he's a living energy too.

I had been working spiritually for a few years and the aura camera became another tool to help me further my spiritual growth. I wasn't to know, at that point, how much influence the aura cam would have and teach me. I will reveal how I started my spiritual pathway in later chapters and remember I never really believed in Guides, Mediums, etc., because I'd always looked at my therapy work as being a science and not spiritual.

Now many years later, I not only work with auras, I teach people all about energy and how to balance their chakras and how to remain balanced by using thought and imagery. When balanced the body is healthy, illness becomes a thing of the past and life brings a new meaning.

So what is an Aura?

Every living being has an electromagnetic field called an "aura". This field vibrates at different frequencies and reflects a person's state of mind, body and being.

The aura is a representation of your thoughts and is continually changing. Every thought you have goes through the chakras and those thoughts are what govern the energy externalised and how you feel inside. If you are very sad and it's a strong heartfelt emotion the heart chakra will enlarge. In its enlarged state it can cause problems with the energy and could break out of the aura or change the auric field enough to externalise an illness. To understand this, all symptoms are caused from within. Every thought has to pass through the chakras. We are total energy and every thought governs the energy the body receives and externalises.

When you understand how chakras work and how thoughts control them, you are on your way to a happy healthy life.

Have you ever been having a pleasant day, feeling energetic, happy, full of life, positive, etc., and then it happens: You meet someone who is feeling low, or down and life isn't good for them. Let me ask you this question: How do you feel after listening to them for five minutes? You don't have to reply because I know the answer, it brings you down and you begin feeling miserable.

We transmit and receive energy all the time and sometimes we can feel the energy in others. With my knowledge of Chakras, energy and how to link into it, I can now pick up on a person's energy very quickly and get an insight into that person, long before the aura camera confirms it. Everyone has this capability and there is no reason why you can't do the same.

I try to keep things simple and not get too complex.

FACT - Everything comes from within you.

FACT - You are and will be what you think.

FACT - You control yourself through your thoughts and your thoughts control the chakras, which in turn, supplies energy to that area, so when balanced and working correctly, everything is fine.

I could go on and on but by now I'm hoping you understand a little more, of course you do. Are you an optimist or a pessimist? The answer should be automatic.

Let me give you another example.

Three people in a hospital ward. All have had the same operation –

One is recovering very slowly, maybe feeling low mentally; the chance of infection is higher.

The second is healing quite well but not yet mobile; there is still a possibility of infection.

The third person heals very quickly indeed because of the positive imagery used and the belief he is going to heal quickly. What the mind perceives in thoughts and images the mind will work towards. This person was out of bed within two days.

The Chakras

What are 'Chakras'? Chakras are the energy centers in our body.

ROOT… BASE Colour: RED - MULADHARA

Located at the base of the spine

This chakra is associated with security, home, money and work. When this chakra is in its clear state the person feels secure. When not in its balanced state, the person may feel insecurity or fear. Strong fear may feel like a threat to survival.

The root chakra represents the Earth and it is the grounding chakra, as in 'Mother Earth', when you're in touch with your roots. It also has strong connections to your own mother. A mother normally supplies the love and food and father supplies the direction. If someone feels a separation from his or her mother, this chakra may be affected until the security is restored in the person's life. The root chakra is connected to the skeleton system and legs, especially the bones. The adrenal glands are also associated with this chakra, as is the nose with the physical sense of smell; also the perception of the physical world: willpower, motivation and intent.

SACRAL… Colour: ORANGE - SVADHISTHANA

Located behind and just below the navel

This chakra is associated with food, sex and pleasure; what the body wants and needs. When this chakra is in its clear state, the person is in touch with communication, listening to and responding appropriately to what the body wants and needs. It's associated with the kidneys, spleen, lower back, adrenal glands and sense of taste and trust. It is also the element of water; if the water is calm and clear, then the energy is balanced, If the water is rough or murky, then the chakra is out of balance and possibly in a conflict. This chakra governs the feelings of sexuality and creativity.

SOLA PLEXUS… Colour: YELLOW - MANIPURA

Located at the V shape formed in the ribcage; above the navel

This chakra is associated with the parts of our consciousness pertaining to perceptions of power, control, or freedom. The element is fire and the gland is the pancreas, the digestive system, liver and bladder. The endocrine gland is associated with the Solar Plexus Chakra. (We could say that diabetics are keeping sweetness from themselves.) This chakra is responsible for the regulation of metabolic energy through digestion. It governs love, compassion and unconditional acceptance of others.

HEART…. Colour: GREEN - ANAHATA

Located midway between shoulder blades (over the sternum)

This chakra is associated with love and compassion, balance and the unconditional acceptance of others. It's associated also with the Thymus gland (immune system), the heart, blood, immune system and also to be able to love as a state of being. The task of this chakra is to integrate and balance the realms of spirit and mind.

THROAT… Colour: BLUE - VISUDDHA

Located in the throat area

The element of this chakra is sound; it is where sound is created. It is associated with communication, expression of thoughts and feelings. The physical organ association is the thyroid and parathyroid glands, lungs, vocal cords and apparatus. It governs communication, expression of thoughts and feelings

THIRD EYE… Colour: INDIGO - AJNA

Located in the centre of the head; behind the forehead

This chakra is associated with the sixth sense and the spiritual realms. It is here we merge with God; a cosmic consciousness; the meaning of life, intuition, visualisation and also clairvoyance. The physical organs are the Pineal gland. This chakra is the link to higher consciousness of God or a higher intelligence. It governs our belief system both conscious and sub-conscious.

CROWN…. Colour: WHITE - SAHASRARA

The Crown chakra is associated with the spiritual realms of higher energy. Enlightenment of knowing this chakra is the link to the outside world of cosmic energy and our concept of what God is. The gland associated with this chakra is the pituitary gland.

These are the seven main chakras but there are many other smaller secondary chakras. But for now we will use these seven.

You now have a brief understanding of the chakras and how they govern everything we do through our thought process. If you think about the heart chakra and see it green and in perfect condition, perfectly round, not expanded in any way, through your own imagery and thought process the mind or subconscious will make it happen. What you visualise will be achieved; FACT but it's like everything else, it takes time and energy to focus. The more you repeat the exercise, the more easily it will become rooted into the subconscious mind; it then becomes something you will do automatically, without even having to think.

Remember learning to ride a bicycle when you were young. How you maybe wobbled a little bit at first, then with balance and practice you became proficient at it. Well, this is what you will be able achieve here. As you learn about the chakras and understand exactly what they are responsible for, you will then come to understand the feelings you experience every day and become proficient at using your mind, thoughts, and imagery to achieve perfect balance within the chakras at all times.

When I am using the aura camera it displays the energy in each chakra live on the screen. It also shows me the external size of the actual aura being projected outwards. This is very beneficial in my work. I learned as much as I could about chakras over many months, closely studying the camera images, printouts, etc. I came to understand how chakras govern and control your body through the thought process. I now felt ready and placed a couple of adverts about the aura camera in my local paper. Before too long I had a booking from a group of women asking for a demonstration and for me to give a talk about my work.

I remember that afternoon as if it were yesterday. My first booking, I was so excited but understandably a little bit nervous.

Of the six women present, four were involved in spiritual work of some kind.

The first woman on the cam was a Reiki Master and the image on the cam came as quite a shock to her. It was showing lots of imbalance in the chakras. It wasn't long before we established why and how this was happening.

I froze the programme and began to print the twenty two-page analysis. As it was printing we turned our attention back to the screen and through imagery and visualisation her chakras were controlled and balanced. Before we began the imagery it was noticeable that the heart, throat, third eye and crown chakra were greatly expanded. The lower part, plexus, sacral and root chakras were very small; in fact, they had virtually no energy.

It was obvious to me what had been happening. Whilst carrying out her healing and working with Reiki she was opening the top four chakras and vibrating very high. The bottom three chakras were closed down. On completion of the Reiki sessions she wasn't closing down the energy in the top chakras and balancing out all seven. They were still open to energy from her spiritual work and she was no longer grounded. There was little wonder she had been experiencing headaches. Around the neck and shoulders was a dark shadow indicating stress. Without the camera I wouldn't have been aware of this but it was live on screen, in front of us both. It was astonishing how similar all the Reiki Masters appeared on the screen.

Whilst they were reading through the aura report the next lady came and sat down. Every chakra displayed was in perfect balance and she was delighted because she taught Yoga and meditation and obviously knew all about her own body's chakras and energy. We had a long chat while I printed her results. She was amazing in what she taught and it certainly showed in her chakras. I could feel it all around her in the auric field; a perfect balance. I would certainly have recommended her to anyone needing to learn relaxation, balance, etc.

I do attend spiritual fairs, demonstrating the aura camera, and whilst in Denia (Spain) a woman came onto the aura camera. All her three top Chakras were massively wide open; displaying lots of energy with dark energy around her shoulders and neck. She was quite distressed and said she had been experiencing severe headaches for months. After a few exercises she balanced the energy in her top chakras. She was watching it live on screen in front of her, experiencing imagery with her eyes open. Once balanced the headache disappeared, completely gone in about four minutes. Many people tell me how easy it is once they understand it. A little guidance and simple exercises is all it takes to balance the chakras

One afternoon, whilst working with a lady the aura cam showed that her throat chakra was hardly visible, virtually closed. The heart chakra, however, was very large with lots of energy around it. What would you think the problem was? The emotion in her heart was very strong and yet the throat chakra energy was so low it pointed to something being held back in her speech. There was lots of emotion needing to be released from the heart area. We chatted for a while and she decided she would like to try hypnosis. Not long into the session the problem emerged. As we continued she kept her hand on the aura camera biosensor and I could see the changes in the chakras as she let go of the emotion. Her throat chakra began to regain its energy and balance, as did the energy in the heart. After another thirty minutes of hypnotherapy and suggestion therapy she was totally balanced and in full control of her thoughts. My client was astounded at the accuracy of the aura camera's twenty-two page analysis. Since the reading she's attended Yoga classes and changed her life for the better. The last time I saw her she was looking much healthy and slimmer, just by taking control of her own energy and thoughts.

Mind, Spirit and Body Fair in the city of Lancaster UK

I was kindly invited to attend the Mind, Spirit and Body Fair to demonstrate my aura camera. Many spiritual people attended, it was and still is a very popular annual event and well attended by the general public. The energy in the room was amazing and I had people queuing for an aura reading. One lady who will always stay in my mind stood in front of me with her husband and quietly said, "Would you possibly do my aura reading please?" She was in her early thirties and very attractive, I would go as far as to say stunning. She sat down on the chair and I took the image, with the energy around her head and shoulders. I froze the programme and whilst the report was printing I took her through the rest of the programme explaining about the chakras and what the machine had picked up on. The lady asked if I could see anything wrong with her. I told her that the energy in the aura picture showed a lot of energy around the solar plexus chakra. In fact, it was showing a very high expanded energy and dark shades were visible on both sides of the aura opposite the chakra. I remember linking very strongly with her energy and would have taken it further and given her a reading but others were waiting to have their aura readings. I did feel a great deal of sadness emanating from her but she sat very quietly, listening intently to the information I had given her.

She and her husband left and I assumed that she had read the report because about fifteen minutes later they reappeared again. I heard her husband say, a few times, go on tell him, let him know.

She sat down next to me and told me that what I had said about the dark shades and the expanded solar plexus chakra was correct. She went on to tell me she was terminally ill with stomach cancer. I was speechless for a few seconds and then said if there was ever anything I could do to help she could call me at any time. It was a very moving experience for me and she came into my thoughts for many months. May her God be with her? The point I would like to stress is the aura cam picked up on it very clearly.

Following are some images I have seen on the aura camera and images of the energy being produced. Look closely and try to envisage what is wrong with the energy. I will also show you a perfect energy balance in the latter pictures. Sorry about the black and white images. When it's live, it's in colour.

A picture of an Aura around Jaqui

As you can see in the picture, the aura is projected around the head and shoulders via the biosensor onto the laptop; the colour was predominantly Blue/Green.

As we learn more about the aura camera and look at actual reports you will have a deeper understanding about energy and what it means. The graphs on the following pages are readings from my wife, taking note that certain chakras are lower than others. It only took about five minutes of working live with the camera, creating imagery and visualisation for her to balance all the chakras and increase her energy.

The biosensor measures and projects stress levels with the balance of mind, body and spirit. It shows the overall vibration and energy level of the chakras and shows your emotional level and state of mind/body link, plus the Yin Yang balance. The chart displays the seven individual chakras and the percentage at which they are working. It also shows a colour wheel. I will explain how this applies later.

The Aura Chakra Bio data Graphs

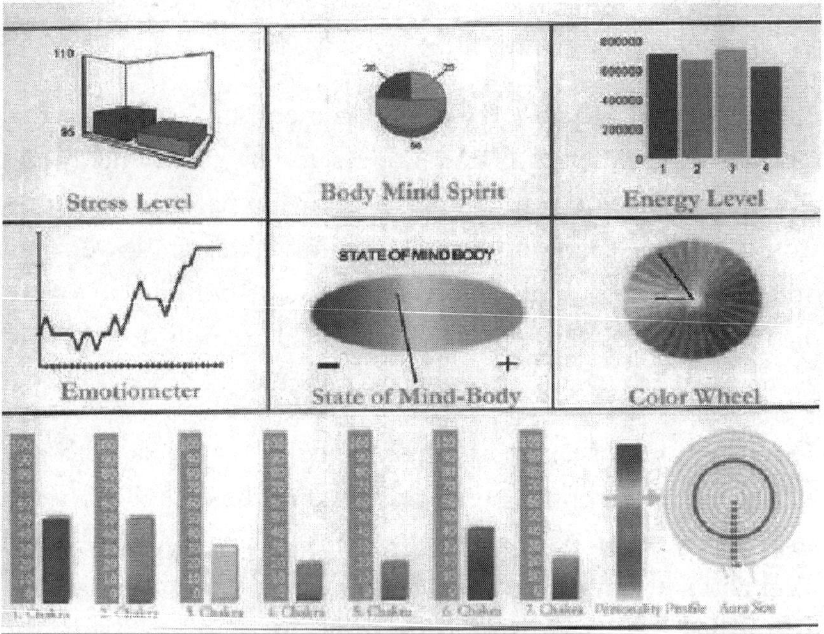

Look at the top left of this picture, here the level of stress has been measured. The scale ranges from 85 at the bottom and goes up to 110+ on the left hand side and the right hand box is reading about 90, indicating some stress, relaxation and balancing needed. Example: 80 represents high physical stress, low circulation, low physical energy.

95 represents average daily physical activity or relaxation level. 110+ represents a high relaxed state and very balanced with high energy

Moving along to the next graph, (middle top)

This is the connection to body, mind and spirit and the graph shows that 50% of the mind is being used, compared to 25%

each of the body and spirit. The mind-body-spirit graph gives you an overview of how your energies are distributed.

The next graph (top right) is the energy level graph and shows the different energy channels that are measured and is based on your electro-dermal activity.

The indigo channel number 1 represents Intuitive Energy.

The green channel number 2 represents Mental Energy

The light blue channel number 3 represents Emotional Energy

The red channel represents Physical Energy

Even bars indicate that the different energy channels are flowing in harmony and each part of your system is vibrating at the same frequency. Uneven bars indicate that there is disharmony or imbalance in the energy flow. This indicates your vibrational rate, starting with lower values from 10,000 to higher values of up to 1,500.000.

Bottom left is the emotion meter and as you see in the graph the lines are quite wavy. This would indicate high emotional stress, high excitement, including nervousness or sensitivity. The ideal image is a straight line showing that the person is stable and centered but may keep emotions inside and may not express them readily.

The bottom middle graph is the connection between mind and body; it is based on your body temperature. Look at the graph, the more the needle is leaning towards the left, the more tense or stressed the person is. The more to the right, the more relaxed and harmonious the person is.

Bottom right is the graph indicating Yin Yang balance. The short needle reflects the female part of you (YIN) and the longer needle is the male (YANG).

Both needles together represent a perfect balance between your left and right side. What you pull in is the same as you give out.

Slightly parted indicates an unbalanced energy between the left-female and right-male and the energies need balancing.

Very apart would indicate a very unbalanced energy. One side of the body may be feeling more tense or stressed. Balancing is highly recommended.

The Chakras

Along the bottom of the graph on page 78 you can see the individual chakras. I will read from left to right starting with the Root chakra; (Red). It's working at about 50% in energy.

The 2nd chakra: Sacral - Orange is about 50% in energy.

The 3rd chakra: Solar Plexus - Yellow, is down at 30% in energy.

The 4th chakra: Heart - Green, is even lower at 20% in energy.

The 5th chakra: Throat - Blue is also low at 20% in energy.

The sixth chakra: Third eye - Indigo, working at around 40% in energy.

The seventh chakra: Crown - White, is working at 20% in energy.

The circle on the right shows the aura energy the body is projecting outwards, thus showing an external energy aura of 50%

I hope you are following and beginning to understand the diagrams. They are showing stress and a lack of energy in many chakras. A session of deep relaxation, imagery and meditation would be recommended to improve the energy in the chakras. Always question to find the reason why the person's energy is so low (cause and effect). As this chart belongs to my wife it was easy for me to understand because it was connected to long hours and stressful situations within her work at school. But the graph is a good example of how energy in the chakras and auric field can drop. It is very much like a battery which has been drained of energy and needs recharging. If your sub-conscious isn't re-energised there could be a possibility of fatigue or illness occurring.

Taking time out and working on the chakras through various imagery techniques, (we will go into these later) my wife had another reading. The chart is shown below. Notice the difference now. It took a maximum of five minutes for her to achieve and get her energies balanced through her chakras.

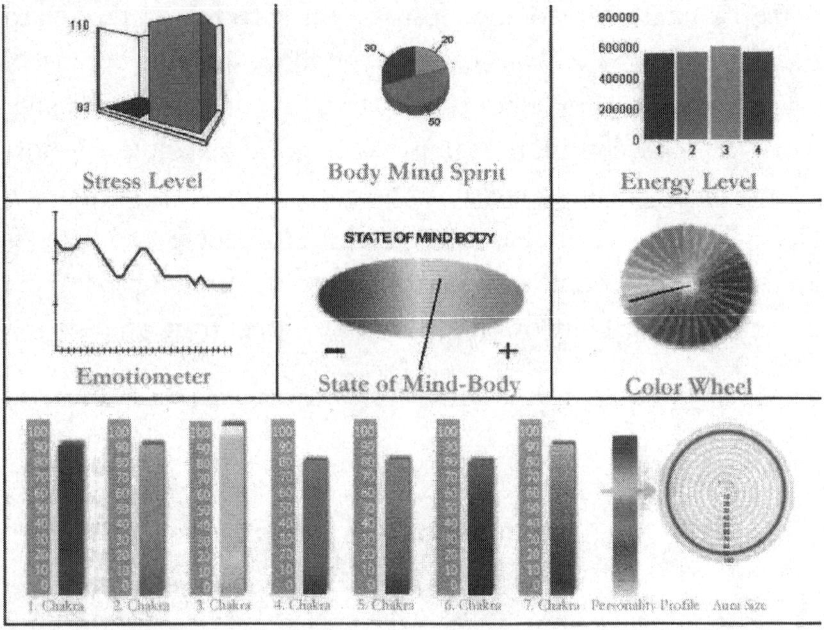

Two charts showing the results, the one below shows a picture of the chakras in the body, notice how round they are and all perfectly balanced.

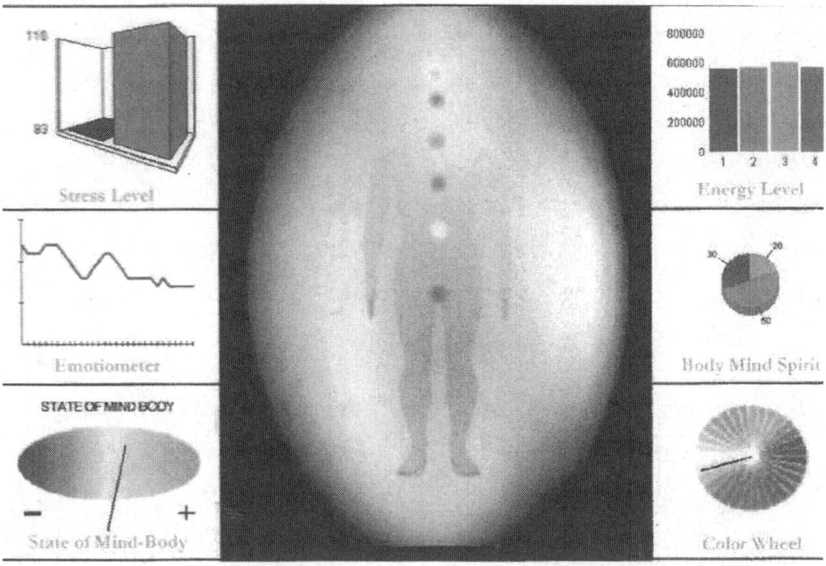

There is a significant difference in the energy in these graphs; the stress level is now much more relaxed. The state of mind and body are more in balance, as shown in the Yin Yang (perfectly balanced) both needles together; and a substantial increase in the chakra energy. The emotion graph is still showing a little bit of concern but of no great importance.

I would normally look for a straight line but as most of the graphs were showing good energy and balance my wife felt no need to continue and felt very relaxed and energised. What she had done was focus on her energy and chakras and let go of all the negative energies she had picked up during her day's work; so many of us never do.

This is a good time to ask: When you get home, do you take ten minutes of relaxation time and charge up the chakras and let go of all the negative energy picked up that day? If you do, **WELL DONE**; if you don't, why not give it a try? It works.

On my old website, via a live recording, you were able to watch how I balanced my own energy. At the time of recording it was very low. To actually see it working speaks volumes. It spares me typing and reiterating what I have tried to explain. It will help you understand much more about how important balance in energy really is.

Over the years of using the aura camera and printing hundreds of aura readings I have yet to be told it was not accurate. People are amazed at its accuracy but we are using a tool that was created by science. Come to think of it, I did once overhear one person say that her reading wasn't right but her friend, who was reading her report with her, kept saying to her, "Yes it is you, and it's so like you." (Smiles) Sometimes we don't like to face the truth but it's the truth within us that will set us free.

So, how to do we balance the chakras?

Imagine the seven chakras in your own body.

See them clearly in your mind.

Start from the root and see a perfect round ball of red light. If there are any blemishes or dark areas clean it using a white light. Clean it, using your mind and imagery until it is clear and pristine.

Move onto the next chakra (yellow), clean it with the white light until that chakra is clear and pristine in your mind.

Move on to the next chakra, then the next until each one is clean, clear and pristine.

Once you have cleaned all the chakras check to make sure each one is in its clear state. You should now feel balanced; it can be as simple as that. When working spiritually the top chakras will be very open to spirit. It is very important when finishing your work to close them down. This is also easy to achieve, using imagery. Imagine them closed, in their normal, round clear, clean, condition. Over the years, with practice I am able to close my chakras very quickly by using a light switch in my mind. I quickly check that all my chakras are in perfect balance, I then just switch off. I know one person, who, when working with spirit, picks up a phone in her mind, does her work and when the session ends puts the phone down, cutting the link. With practice, you will find your own method of closing but it is very important to close the energy after working spiritually.

Even whilst I am walking or watching television I can check my chakras with my eyes open. Never try this with your eyes closed, unless it's safe to do so, sit in a chair or somewhere you can relax. This also works for raising energy when feeling low, as per the example earlier of my wife and the diagrams we went through.

Many years ago, when I was learning about hypnosis, I recorded a C/D for balancing the chakras. Although, at that time, I had very little knowledge of chakras, it just seemed like a pleasant recording to chill out and relax to. The C/D takes you on a journey through the chakras by using hypnosis and guidance into a very deep state of relaxation.

The journey takes you to a mountain where there are seven terraces carved into the side. The mountain is colourful and there is a garden on each terrace and each garden has a colour which stretches into the clouds.

The journey uses the colour of each chakra. Imagery and affirmations at each terrace guide you up through the chakras creating balance and harmony within yourself. Beginning with the first garden, which is red, continuing up through the chakras until you are in the white garden and then beyond. Email me via my website and I will send you a free copy. Ask for the Seven Terraces MP3.

Children have amazing auras

Below is an aura of a young girl. Just notice the energy around her. You would certainly feel this energy if you were sat near her as she displays a very positive outlook in life which in turn projects a very large and positive aura. Children are brilliant to work with and this young girl is just going to be awesome in years to come.

Many years ago a friend sent me this and it's simply amazing how accurate it is:

Explanations of the Colour in Any Aura

Red Aura

What are Red Auras and what does it mean to have red as one of the dominant colours of the Aura?

The Aura colour that surrounds an individual reflects their personality and points to their future destiny.

Red Aura people are enthusiastic and energetic individuals, forever on the lookout for new adventures. They are adventurous with food, travel and sexual partners. The mantra of the Red Aura colour individual is "I'll try anything once." Because of their devil-may-care approach to life they often find themselves in hot water.

Red Aura people are quick to anger and can lose their temper over the slightest thing. But on the upside they are generous with their time and energy when called upon for help.

They are normally strong in body and mind and do not succumb to physical or mental illness easily. Because of their robust health and fitness the Red Aura individual likes to be physical and will excel in sports. People with a predominant red Aura colour can easily become bored and need to move on to different interests, projects and relationships because then they leave lots of unfinished ventures in their wake. But if they set their mind to a project and can stick to it, they will have remarkable success and can become extremely wealthy.

Red Aura people are direct, to the point and forthright and are not afraid to make their point of view heard. They don't normally have hidden agendas or ulterior motives. What you see is what you get with the open and up front Red Aura individual.

Above all else the Red Aura individual needs to be number one. Their competitive nature and need to succeed will drive them towards great success in life. They are not good team players and won't take orders from others. They will prefer to run their own one man business or be in positions of authority over others.

Yellow Aura

What are Yellow Auras and what does it mean to have Yellow as one of the dominant colours of the Aura?

Yellow Aura people are analytical, logical and very intelligent. They tend to excel in careers that involve teaching and study and make excellent inventors and scientists. They can have a tendency to work too hard and can easily become a workaholic putting their work above personal relationships.

Yellow Aura people are perfectly happy in their own company and do not suffer loneliness. They are prone to mental health pressures, though and can become withdrawn and depressed when stressed.

The Yellow Aura individual is a brilliant communicator and can display their skills on a one to one basis and in front of large crowds. They are confident in their abilities to get their ideas and messages across and will inspire others.

Yellow Aura people have very good observation skills and can read people easily. They possess extremely good perception. Because they do not suffer fools gladly and will choose their few friends carefully. Any friends they do have will need to match the Yellow Aura person's wit and intellect.

The Yellow Aura individual tends to put their head above their heart when faced with difficult choices and decision making. They are unorthodox and unconventional thinkers and not afraid to experiment with different ideas and original concepts. To some the Yellow Aura seems a little eccentric with unusual interests and hobbies. They are attracted to anything which is considered avant-garde, intellectual or unusual.

The main fault of a person who has a predominant Yellow Aura is that they can be overly critical of themselves and others.

Pink Aura

What are Pink Auras and what does it mean to have pink as one of the dominant colours of the Aura?

Pink Aura people are by nature loving and giving. They love to be loved too, they gather around them close friends and family at every opportunity. They like to host family events and are very generous of their time. They have a high regard for their health and will look after their bodies with good diet, nutrition and exercise.

Pink Aura people are very romantic and once they have found their soulmate will stay faithful, loving and loyal for life.

The Pink Aura individual is a natural healer, highly sensitive to the needs of others and has strong psychic abilities. They also have very creative ideas and strong imaginations. Because of these personality traits, the Pink Aura person makes great writers of novels, poetry or song lyrics.

The Pink Aura individual hates injustice, poverty and conflicts. They strive always to make the world a better place and will make personal sacrifices in the pursuit of this ideal.

Pink Aura people are strong willed and highly disciplined and will expect high standards from others. They have strong values and morals and seldom deviate from them. Because of their honesty and likable nature they are valued as employees but also make excellent employers because of their sense of fairness.

Green Aura

Green Aura people are highly creative and very hard working. They strive for perfection in everything they do. They have a very determined and down to earth nature and will not allow fanciful dreams and unrealistic ideas to colour their world.

Their creativity takes the form of practical matters such as gardening, cooking and home decorating. The Green Aura individual has a fine eye for beauty and will ensure their appearance and clothing, home and surroundings are both practical and beautiful.

Green Aura people tend to be very popular, admired and respected. They make for very successful business people and can create much wealth and prosperity for themselves. Green Aura people like security, stability and balance in their lives.

Any plans they make a well thought out and because this, they seldom make rash mistakes.

Close friends of Green Aura people will be treated to generosity, loyalty and practical advice. Green Aura people do not suffer fools gladly and choose their friends very carefully. People with a predominant green Aura tend to be rather health-conscious and ensure their diet is nutritious; health giving and tasty. They are always in tune with nature and love the great outdoors.

Orange Aura

Orange Aura people are gregarious, generous, social souls. They love to be in the company of others and don't mind being the center of attention or just another face in the crowd. They want to please others and are often the best gift givers, being very thoughtful and generous.

The Orange Aura individual is normally goodhearted, kind and honest. They are very in tune to the emotions of others and can sense and feel their pain and joy. Orange Aura people can be very charming, but part of their charm is in their sensitivity to others. They have the ability to make everyone feel at ease in their company.

The Orange Aura individual can be hot headed and quick to lose their temper. But on the positive side they are equally quick to forgive and forget if a sincere apology is offered and accepted. They do not hold grudges.

Orange Aura people are confident of the impression they make on others and can use this to their advantage. They tend to lead very successful and happy lives. On the down side,

Orange Aura people tend to be impatient and tend to rush into projects, relationships and experiences too quickly. They normally tend to act immediately and consider the consequences later.

Purple Aura

Purple Aura people are highly psychic, attuned to the emotions and moods of others and very sensitive. People who have a predominant amount of purple in their Aura are seen as mysterious and secretive.

The Purple Aura individual possesses a philosophical, enquiring and intuitive mind. They love to learn and never stop exploring and enquiring into new subjects and areas that interest them. Because this they tend to be extremely interesting and knowledgeable people.

The Purple Aura individual does not have a wide circle of many friends. But the friends they do have are held close and are respected, admired and loved. People with a predominant purple Aura tend to be unlucky in love but once they have found their perfect soul mate is loyal and loving for life.

Purple Aura people connect well with animals and nature. They are attuned to animals and can sense their emotions and feelings. Purple Aura people tend to take in and care for strays as their loving and caring nature makes it difficult for them to turn strays away.

Blue Aura

Having a predominant blue Aura or energy field surrounding you can point to a number of personality traits. Totally blue

Auras are quite rare but can show up as one of the boldest Aura colours in people with strong personalities.

Blue Aura people are the master communicators of the world. They have the ability to convey their thoughts, ideas, views and concepts eloquently and charismatically. They make for excellent writers, poets and politicians.

Blue Aura people are also highly intelligent and very intuitive. They certainly have the head and heart balanced in making difficult decisions and choices. They are incredibly good organisers and can motivate and inspire others.

People who have a predominant amount of blue in their Auras are peacemakers and have the ability to calmly smooth out angry situations. They prize truthfulness, direct communication and clarity in all their relationships. The downside of the Blue Aura personality is that they can take on too much, become workaholics and neglect their personal relationships.

White Aura / Silver Aura

White/Silver Aura people are exceptionally gifted. How they use their gifts wisely is their life lesson. White/Silver Aura individuals are bestowed with sensitivity, intuitiveness, psychic ability and practicality. They can use their spiritual understanding in very practical ways. Because this they can relate to many people and are often found in teaching, mentoring or counselling careers.

White/Silver Aura people have immense versatility and adaptability and are capable of getting the most out of virtually every opportunity in life. Their high intellect enables then to make the right decisions quickly and follow through with action.

People who have predominant silver Auras are seen as very attractive. They attract many admirers. But White/Silver Aura people are very discerning and choose their friends carefully and their lovers very carefully.

White/Silver Aura people tend to be well blessed in looks, personality and talent and as such are seen as incredibly lucky people. Success seems to come easily to White/Silver Aura people.

6. Being Spiritual

Many of us seem to think that being spiritual means we have to be religious. Just because you are not directly connected with a specific religion, doesn't mean you shouldn't strive to become more spiritual. I was raised without any form of religion whatsoever. The whole concept of spiritual awareness isn't just about connecting with a higher divine power but also connecting with yourself and nature. Once you have established this connection, you will see life from a totally different perspective. People with a highly developed sense of spiritual awareness are often less prone to depression, addiction, manipulation, and control. In addition, they generally understand what it means to be truly happy.

Learn to Communicate With Your Soul

Your soul is an energy entity that holds part of your awareness and memories. Its energy is that animates your body. In other words, your physical body acts like a vehicle to house your soul so that it can experience what it means to live in the material world. For these reasons your soul is your true identity. Your body isn't your true identity because it's made of matter, made of atoms which are mostly empty spaces. The space that isn't empty in the atoms isn't solid but is actually made of energy. So what does this mean? It means that matter and your body are more like illusions or projections. The only thing that is truly real is energy, which is what your soul is made of. To communicate with your soul, you need to first believe that you have one. Next, learn how to calm your mind so that you can hear the subtle voice and feeling inside you. A great way to calm your mind is to meditate. This is another great technique to strengthen your ability to communicate to your soul.

Get Plenty of Sleep

Create a schedule that makes it possible for you to get at least six to eight hours of sleep every night. Once you have created this schedule, try to stick to it. Not only will you find that getting lots of sleep every single night allows your body to recover from fatigue but you are also making it easier for you to focus your thoughts. Staying in control of your thoughts is important for increasing your spiritual awareness because thought is the energy entity that constructs your reality.

Spend Time with Nature

The secrets of life are embedded in nature. If you want to increase your spiritual awareness to be able to understand what life is, you need to study nature and learn how to live in harmony with it. As your connection to nature strengthens, your spiritual awareness will also increase. The reason for this is when you become more aware of your natural environment, you start to see why things occur the way they do. This awareness can help you understand who you are and why you are here.

This section I would like to share with you all: 12 Tips for Recovering from Emotional Pain

By: Luminita D. Saviuc

Pain *(any pain–emotional, physical, mental) has a message. The information it has about our life can be remarkably specific, but it usually falls into one of two categories: "We would be more alive if we did more of this," and, "Life would be lovelier if we did less of that." Once we get the pain's message, and follow its advice, the pain goes away."*

~ Peter McWilliams

Have you noticed how afraid we all are of feeling any emotional pain? And how we would do anything in our power to avoid it? Nobody wants it. We all try to get rid of it. We all try to hide and run away from it, and the irony is that the more we try to reject and resist it, the more intense it gets and the longer it stays with us.

We all have our ups and downs. We all experience emotional pain from time to time. But that doesn't mean there's something wrong with us. It doesn't mean we're 'broken' or 'defective'. On the contrary. It only shows that we are human. That we have feelings and emotions.

Today I would like to share with you 12 tips for recovering from emotional pain. So that you can continue living your life in peace and harmony and do the things you so much enjoy doing.

1. EMBRACE WITH GRACE ALL THAT YOU FACE.

"Everything you are against weakens you. Everything you are for empowers you."

~ Wayne Dyer

Let go of any feelings of anger, disgust or frustration you might have towards yourself, your emotional pain and your current reality. Resist nothing. Embrace with grace all that you face. Surrender to what is. Accept what you are going through. All your thoughts, feelings and frustrations. Accept your emotional pain as if you have chosen it.

2. GIVE YOURSELF TIME.

It takes time to drive out the darkness from our minds and our hearts. It takes time to accept the presence of emotional pain into our lives. So give yourself time. Time to rest, time to heal and time to fully recover. Be gentle with yourself and trust that everything happens exactly as it's supposed to happen.

3. LET GO OF CONTROL.

"There is a time for being ahead, a time for being behind; a time for being in motion, a time for being at rest; a time for being vigorous, a time for being exhausted; a time for being safe, a time for being in danger. The Master sees things as they are, without trying to control them. She lets them go their own way, and resides at the centre of the circle."

~ Lao Tzu, Tao Te Ching

Please refrain yourself from making comments like: "I have been feeling like this for far too long. I should be fine by now. Why does it take so long for this pain to be gone?" and so on. Allow things to follow their natural course. Allow yourself to heal at your own pace. Let go of the need to control the healing process. Let go of the need to speed up your recovery.

4. SUFFER CONSCIOUSLY.

Observe your emotional pain, your anguish and frustrations. Observe the constant stream of negative thoughts that run through your mind. The dreadful stories that keep feeding your pain, but choose not to identify yourself with them. See yourself as the one who's observing all that emotional pain and all that discomfort. But don't make the pain part of who you are. Don't make it your person life story. Don't claim it as your own.

"Suffering consciously is when you feel, sense and accept the suffering. It is not suffering anymore, it is just pain. To be suffering you must have an unhappy me with a story and the world that is doing it to me."

~ Eckhart Tolle

5. LOVE YOUR PAIN AWAY.

Nobody likes to be in the presence of pain. We all want to get rid of it. To run as far away from it as we possibly can. But there are times when pain demands our presence, our focus and attention. There are times when pain demands to be felt. So take the time to know your emotional pain. To nourish it is to understand it. Don't curse your pain. Love your pain and it will go away.

"Darkness cannot drive out darkness; only light can do that. Hate cannot drive out hate; only love can do that."

~ Martin Luther King

6. GIVE TIME, TIME.

"Time heals almost everything. Give time, time."

~ Regina Brett

It takes time to drive out the darkness from our minds and from our hearts. It takes time to heal our wounds and accept the presence of emotional pain into our lives. So give time, time for it to heal.

7. SPEND TIME ALONE WITH YOURSELF.

When you love someone, you spend private time with that person, quality time. And in the dark moments of our lives, when pain is present in our hearts and in our minds, spending time alone with ourselves is one of the best gift we can give to ourselves.

Take the time to be alone with yourself. To acknowledge, love and appreciate the parts of you that are beautiful. To love yourself and to know yourself. To rest, time to heal and to fully recover from all that you are feeling.

"Your light is seen, your heart is known, your soul is cherished by more people than you might imagine. If you knew how many others have been touched in wonderful ways by you, you would be astonished. If you knew how many people feel so much for you, you would be shocked. You are far more wonderful than you think you are. Rest with that. Rest easy with that. Breathe again. You are doing fine. More than fine. Better than fine. You're doing' great. So relax. And love yourself today."

~ Neale Donald Walsch

8. REACH OUT FOR HELP AND SUPPORT.

"Surround yourself with people who make you happy. People who make you laugh, who help you when you're in need. People who genuinely care. They are the ones worth keeping in your life. Everyone else is just passing through."

~ Karl Marx (composer)

Reach out for emotional help and support from those you love and trust. Surround yourself with cheerful and happy people. People who can make you laugh, who can make you see how beautiful life is and who can show you that there's always something to look forward to.

9. LET NATURE HEAL AND COMFORT YOU.

"One has to be alone, under the sky, before everything falls into place and one finds his or her own place in the midst of it all. We have to have the humility to realise ourselves as part of nature."

~ Thomas Merton

Spend more time outdoors and Look outside in nature for evidence of decay, destruction and death. Of rebirth, rejuvenation, and renewal. And remind yourself that you too are part of nature. Allow nature to be your wise friend, teacher and companion. Allow nature to heal and comfort you. To teach you more about the infinite circle of life. About birth, life, death, rebirth and about yourself.

10. CLAIM NOTHING AS YOUR OWN.

Love everything but cling on to nothing. Make peace with this idea that nothing in this life lasts forever, that nothing is yours to keep. Live each day as if it were your last. Each moment as if it were your only moment. Make the best of everything life sends your way and waste no time on arguing against what is.

"Most of our troubles are due to our passionate desire for and attachment to things that we misapprehend as enduring entities."

~Dalai Lama

"A person who lives moment to moment, who goes on dying to the past, is never attached to anything. Attachment comes from the accumulated past. If you can be unattached to the past every moment, then you are always fresh, young, just born. You pulsate with life and that pulsation gives you immortality. You are immortal, only unaware of the fact."

~ Osho

11. TURN YOUR WOUNDS INTO WISDOM.

Every experience that comes your way, comes your way for a reason. Seek to know what that reason is. Seek to learn from every painful experience and every painful interaction life sends your way. Be an alchemist. Turn your wounds into wisdom and your difficulties into opportunities. Let your pain make you better, not bitter.

"Out of clutter, find simplicity. From discord, find harmony. In the middle of difficulty lies opportunity."

~ Albert Einstein

12. NO PAIN IS FOREVER.

If you're still alive, if you're still breathing, it only means that there's still a lot of life for you out there. A lot of places for you to go to, many new and exciting things to do, to learn and to love. So pick yourself up, dust yourself off and start all over again. Start rebuilding your life and make it ridiculously amazing. Don't let a bad and painful experience make you feel like you have a bad and painful life. Don't let a rainy day dampen your fun. Never forget that the Sun always shines above the clouds. It's always up there.

"Our real blessings often appear to us in the shape of pains, losses and disappointments; but let us have patience and we soon shall see them in their proper figures."

~ Joseph Addison

Later in this book I will show you a different way to remove and neutralise painful memories, etc

7. Spirit Guides

I didn't realize at the beginning of my journey I had been healing in many ways through my hypnotherapy work. I wasn't aware of my own spirituality until I met my guide Joshua. I was a sceptic with regard to guides and angels, people who could 'talk to the dead' (people who had passed over into 'Spirit') and were relaying messages to members of their family. But the truth was I was scared of it, as so many people are, so I dismissed it. A number of years passed and I regularly visited my chosen rooms on the internet. I would sit and listen to Mediums, Clairvoyants, Tarot card readers and many others who worked in various ways with spirit. These were found in the Metaphysical and Spiritual room section. It wasn't long before I created my own room discussing 'Past Lives' and in that room I met many wonderful people. People discussing all areas of spirituality, one in particular talking about guides and their function in people's lives on the earth plane. I had Mediums giving readings and connecting amazingly with others in the room. I had been told, many years previously, that I would be doing similar work in my future but back then I very much doubted it; I was comfortable with my hypnotherapy and past life work. The Aura camera wasn't on the scene at that particular time.

A few years passed and one day whilst I was undertaking stonework in an area in the Lake District. U.K., something was about to take place that would change my life forever.

I worked as a stonemason and dry stone-waller for many years and have built and repaired thousands of meters of dry stone walls. I have converted old barns into homes, stone faced new-build houses and created fancy stone fireplaces.

My friend and I were working on a stretch of wall which was in a dangerous state of repair. I was inspecting and marking out the sections that had begun to bulge inwards, towards the field. This was due to the increase in the size and volume of vehicles causing vibrations and movement in the wall. It was only being held together by years and years of growth from bracken and briers entwined into and through it.

My friend was about 100 yards away in his small digger, using the front bucket to pull down the parts I had marked for repair. As I continued to remove some of the growth and check the state of repair of the wall I came across a very old hand carved stone gate stoop; the craftsmanship was impressive. It had been there for goodness knows how many years, possibly a hundred. I hoped, by using the machine, we might be able to remove it in one piece. A stone stoop of this size was in demand and would have cost a great deal of money to purchase.

As I turned around away from the wall I had the experience of being pushed from behind. I was pushed very hard, on my left shoulder. The push was harsh and it sent me hurtling forward and as I fell towards the ground the stone slab I had been looking at only seconds before, SLAMMED onto the ground next to me; brushing my side as it landed. It hit the ground with such a force the ground around me shuddered. I turned around to yell at my friend for pushing me so hard but couldn't believe he was fifty meters away, sitting in his cab, staring towards me, his mouth wide open in disbelief.

He came running over and asked me how I knew that the stone slab was falling towards me, as I had my back to it. He thought I was about to be crushed and there was nothing he could have done as he was so far away. I told him that I thought he had pushed me out of the way. I was shaking from head to foot. I kept getting flashes in my mind, all afternoon. Flashes of a very dark person, someone very tall, a strange type of energy kept coming into me for most of the afternoon; something I had never experienced before. I knew I wasn't over reacting but I just couldn't seem to stop shaking. I also felt a little nauseated but I simply put it down to shock. After all I could have been seriously injured or even killed.

That evening I went onto the internet and opened my past life regression room and as if by magic a person came into my room and asked if I was okay. It was Mag's, "Happymags", she had picked up on my energy and vibrations immediately and was very aware that something was happening to me and offered to help me.

I accepted without question and spent a few hours in a private room working with her and connecting more to the guide who was trying to connect with me. She taught me how to open up my crown chakra and let the guide come through. I could see the imagery so clearly and when I was asked his name, my reply was automatic. He's called Joshua but Josh for short and he's six foot seven inches tall. He was stood next to a bench at the entrance of what seemed like a totally different country, something I had never seen before and I felt that I had experienced many lives before with him. His skin was as black as the night and he was wearing what looked like a dark brown suit. I knew and sensed he was from Egypt. He was a very jovial character walking up and down laughing. He had tried connecting with me many, many times before but I was far too stubborn and simply not ready but at long last he was through. In the early days working with Josh he would always sit on the bench, cross his legs, then bring forward a relative from the past, as a form of closure or indication of the connection we had together. This imagery was very intense. That first evening was very emotional, especially when he brought both my parents through. It was like they were right with me.

As I'm typing about him, he's become visible in my thoughts and I can see him, quite clearly, sitting on the bench, smiling as usual, and trying his very best to distract me.

Since that enlightening experience, there's hardly a day passes when I don't have Josh in my thoughts. He's been with me now for a very long time, guiding me through areas of my life, both good and bad. Sometimes though he simply leaves it up to me to sort out and doesn't get involved. My own Free Will.

I didn't really know much about guides then, only the little knowledge picked up whilst hearing others talk in my room; and here I am, with my very own guide. Spirit will do all they can to help you connect but you have to open the top chakras and go higher in vibration for them to connect to you. Through practice I am able to connect very easily now, (remember the light switch). It can be as simple as that and I have learned to always ask for permission before I connect; I feel it's only right and the polite thing to do. If Josh has anything for me he usually lets me know he's around. I then take the time and sit down with him on the bench, the bench in my imagery. I don't always connect immediately, sometimes it can take as long as a day before I can connect to him, other times it is much quicker.

After a year or so I began to experience strange vibrations again but couldn't really connect with what I was feeling. I asked for Josh to assist me, which he did. Before long another guide came through, it was my Grandfather from my native past life; (Nahkoma) it was an honour and privilege to have him come through and it wasn't long before I was working with both guides.

Nahkoma was and still is a very wise, native elder who gave me guidance and direction.

When I work with him we always go to the open fire where he sits and we stare into the flames as he talks and gives me guidance. I've had so many nights with him enjoying the images he brings to me. I have even had friends join me in my room on the internet. I relay to them what is happening as Nahkoma and I sit round the fire. His wisdom is vast and for me he brings me heart felt energy and grounding. He always comes to me whenever I'm using empathy in my work. He helps me connect to the aura energy and vibration around heart felt issues my client may be experiencing. Both Josh and Nahkoma have been incredible in my growth. I didn't know when I was working with Josh I could have several guides but within three months I found myself connecting to yet another guide.

This gentleman came in very slowly and had great energy around his head. He was bringing a connection for me to go spiritually higher in my work and for me to raise my vibrations. This guides name was 'Natulta' and he came from Atlantis. Please don't ask me how I knew this, I just did. I knew very little about Atlantis at that particular time and it's only over years of reading and researching that I understand a little more about the lost city of Atlantis. The reason he came was to teach me how to accept spirit more easily and to accept my first judgment of the images I received. He was responsible for teaching me how to open my crown chakra and link to the universal energy which I now use regularly. I was now working with three guides and at times it became very confusing as to who was coming through. I decided, one night, to ask Josh to give me a sign that it was him; he sent ice cold shivers right down my legs. I always know when he is connecting to me because I get the same cold shivers. I asked Nahkoma to give me a sign and he warmed my heart area with a glowing energy and lovely relaxed feeling. Natulta came right to the top of my head and gave me so much energy at times I could go quite dizzy. I could now tell which one was guiding me and when.

I had been working with all my guides for about a year or slightly longer when I noticed that I wasn't able to connect with Josh anymore. All I could do was see him in my mind but I knew it was just my imagery and it wasn't him in a spiritual sense. I continued with my two other guides but was a little saddened at not being able to see Josh anymore. Perhaps he had done all he was meant to do for me and had moved on to help someone else. Over the next four months I worked with Grandfather and Natulta; it was a strange four months in my growth. Suddenly one evening whilst I was at home, watching television, Josh came back into my mind, this time I knew it was real because my legs were getting an icy cold energy in them.

I closed my eyes and went straight over to our bench. He was beaming and smiling from ear to ear. He had come to give me some good news and to let me know what he had been up to and where he had been. He told me that he was now my 'Gate Keeper' and had been away to be counselled for his new position. I didn't know what he meant by 'Gatekeeper'. It brought back memories of school, history, medieval times and castles; but it was great to have him back.

Apparently, his purpose was now to protect me and only let good spiritual energy through the gate. A good friend told me what the purpose of a gatekeeper was; it was the same explanation I received directly from Josh. Uncanny or what?

Over the years, in my room on the internet I have had many very knowledgeable guest speakers who were able to explain more about spiritual protection. Anything from a 'white' energy around you to being encapsulated in a protective bubble of spiritual energy. I had never heard anything like this before. The only protection I had been given were shields in my wrists. This was for protection when I am carrying out my healing work with my hands and working with the universal energy of spirit. I will explain and tell you more about why I was given the shields later.

Natulta had been with me for a while and I now know he had been helping me use my crown chakra (my pineal gland or third eye) to develop and increase the link to universal energy; especially for the healing work I was now doing. Without his guidance, I am sure I would not be as capable as I am now. I feel he has now moved on to teach others, because after he had taught me, he left fairly quickly. I often smile and give thanks for the wonderful teaching he gave me. Who knows maybe one day he will return.

I was now left with two guides and they have stayed with me for a very long time. I am still working with them and enjoying every day, as each day brings new challenges. It hasn't always been like this and it hasn't always been easy. Most days bring in new movements and directions in my spiritual work and guidance which is essential for my future growth.

Linking with universal energy wasn't accessible to me for many years. It is only since living in Spain that the connection became stronger and more direct. I was aware of the healing capabilities and I used them on many occasions in the UK but possibly it was more ego rather than spirituality. I wasn't really aware of how strong the energy was becoming.

Twenty-six years ago Jaqui, Simon, my son and I went to live in Spain. I was going to set up and work as a hypnotherapist. Everything was very difficult and the rules and regulations in Spain, at that time, were very complex and to some extent, still are. We lived inland from Denia on the East Coast and rented a spacious, three bedroom, detached villa; with a fabulous view over acres of orange groves.

Things were going fairly smoothly and my therapy side, although slow to start, began to grow, but the funds were getting low. The two people in who we had put our trust, stayed with and had gone to Spain to work with, turned the experience into an utter nightmare. We had been told a complete pack of lies and the relationship soon broke down. We closed the door and has it never been reopened since. The decision to return to the UK happened one day whilst we were shopping at a local supermarket. My wife made a long, awaited phone call home (it was quite expensive calling England then) and was told that her father was very poorly. We sat, discussed, and debated the best course of action for us to take. Within a few days we had booked our flights home and it wasn't long before we returned to England. It happened so fast but looking back, at the time it was the right thing to do. My wife who was very close to her father was able to be there for him. Was I guided back by my guides? I think so.

We have always loved Spain and often talked about going back one day to semi retire. The closest we got were a few snatched holidays in Benidorm. We always enjoyed being back, enjoying the Spanish culture and of course the lovely sunshine.

Now, some twenty-five plus years later I was back living in Spain, once again and my wife was sorting things out in the UK and hopefully, soon to join me for good. She stayed with me during the school holidays, sometimes a few weeks at a time. We had been apart for several months and being apart from each other made us both more determined to continue on our spiritual journey and therapy work.

On the 2nd of March (Mother's day) 2009 I returned to Spain. I flew into Alicante airport to begin a new life in Benidorm. I wanted to set up a small business carrying out my therapy, aura cam work, hypnotherapy, past lives and my spiritual work. I had a certain amount of money saved to pay for my rent and to survive for up to six months, until hopefully my work would be bringing in an income for both of us. Jaqui would remain in the UK and look after our home and continue her work as Head of a 'Behaviour Support Centre' at a local school. She would join me once I had an income to support us both but would spend school holidays with me in Spain. Our home in the UK would be taken care of by our son, Simon. We had decided not to sell it, just in case we ever wanted to return, as it was our financial security should we ever need it.

I rented a ninth floor apartment in Benidorm, overlooking the famous Poniente beach area, where there was always a beautiful clear blue sea and blue skies. It was a three bedroom, two-bathroom apartment with double front facing terrace with an amazing view of the port and the whole of the bay. My rent was fully paid until the end of May. The day I arrived the temperature was 22C with a sunny, cloudless, blue sky and I was able to spend quiet time on the terrace at nights working with Josh and Nahkoma

Soon, this would all change.

Every day I found that I needed more information before I was legally allowed to work in Spain. I needed an 'E' number, this I had to get from the local police station. I queued every day, for three days, outside the building, in sweltering heat, with little or no shade. There seemed to be hundreds of people, all waiting and this was just for the forms. Once the form was completed there was a three week waiting period before it was returned; every move in Spain costs money. I was walking everywhere, I walked miles each day. Things were becoming very complex. I believed I would get work easily, well it just wasn't happening.

My back and legs ached terribly, with all the walking each day but I also felt that something was wrong. I would visit hotels seeking permission to demonstrate my aura camera but I got the same answer from them all. They all wanted to charge me a massive amount of commission. I could never have seen enough people through the day to break even. All my plans were backfiring. On the third week in March the weather turned bad; lots of rain with very heavy winds. The winds were turning the sand into a very fine powder and I could taste it in my mouth and the back of my throat. It got everywhere. The apartment was covered in a fine layer of gritty sand, it got into my lungs and gave me a very bad chest infection. I was so ill one night I just wanted to get to hospital, I dialled 999 then tried 911 but of course they were the wrong numbers for Spain. I managed to get a little sleep amongst the severe coughing bouts. The next morning I walked to a local bar to get something to eat; I had not eaten for two days. It was there I met Geoff who told the name of a medicine to help me with the chest infection and within three days, of taking a course of antibiotics and medicine for the chest infection; I was and felt much better.

I know it was my guides who directed me to that bar because I had no idea it was there. I went on a regular basis after that and became good friends with the owners. One morning whilst I was having my breakfast, at that very same bar, (this will remain with me forever and taught me so much), I met a man in a wheelchair; we sat together having a coffee and chat. I wrongly assumed, because he was in a wheel chair that he was disabled. I found out during our conversation, that one night, two weeks prior, whilst he was on his way home a little worse for wear; in fact, quite inebriated, he had been mugged and very badly beaten up. We chatted for a long time and he was very interested in my aura cam work and hypnotherapy. He had used hypnosis for the pain in his back many years ago and was interested in using it again. Dave was also a very spiritual person and a good conversationalist. We spent a pleasant couple of hours together. He was the first person I had talked to in Spain regarding my therapy work.

You will see later why I do not believe in the word coincidence. Instead I say: Everything happens for a reason.

Later that day I noticed a small advert in a shop widow, it read - Mind Body Spirit festivals in Spain and within minutes I was speaking to the girl who organised the events. I booked a place for myself and my aura camera for the forthcoming fairs. My first fair would be the following month in Denia. How strange, as twenty years earlier I lived very close to Denia and spent many lovely hours there. That word coincidence nearly came back. The fair was a huge success for me and I met lots of spiritual people over the two days.

Suddenly there seemed a light at the end of the tunnel, but it was still difficult without any form of transport and one evening whilst on the phone to Jaqui I suggested that I got a 125cc motor scooter; everyone uses them in Spain.

Well, at least I would be able to get around easier. Even buying a scooter was complex. A document of registration is required to prove that you are living in Spain, a rent contract and a certificate stamped by the local town hall are also requirements before you can buy a car or scooter in Spain. Documents must be carried with you at all times, including your insurance, driving license, vehicle registration and a bank receipt, proof of payment. I remember the conversation so well on the phone to Jaqui. She said, "No-way, I'm not coming on it". I wasn't really surprised because throughout our married life she wouldn't allow me to get a motor bike because of a nasty experience she'd had many years previously.

Three weeks later I was the proud owner of a brand new scooter. Oh, bliss, no more trudging the streets. At last I could go exploring and find my way around. I was the answer to Spain's Hells Angels. Well, not really.

Jaqui came for the midterm holiday. It took me a little while to persuade her to get on the back of the scooter. After that she wanted to go everywhere on it; she said, "it's like being free and of course the beautiful weather makes all the difference".

I was now able to get around Benidorm much easier. It was fun in the good weather meeting and chatting to people about my work. I did get some aura cam and past life work from the tourists but it simply wasn't enough to pay for everything, but it was a start and I loved it.

I had to think about finding another apartment. I needed to move at the end of May as my rent contract expired. Whilst on her break from school, Jaqui and I found an ideal location, just north of Benidorm, called La Nucia. I rented a secure walled Villa with its own pool and hotbox and it was much cheaper than the apartment on the Poniente. Jaqui would be over for the last week of May on her half term break to help me move. I began to feel a little low as far as work was concerned. I would run out of money if the work didn't come in soon. I certainly hadn't planned on spending 1,500 Euros on a scooter, but it was either buy it or struggle walking everywhere, but it reduced my funds greatly. (Ouch)

One evening I was having a drink, overlooking the Port, sat on my terrace, just chilling out. One drink became two, one more and then another one and I became quite 'worse for wear'. I was getting myself into quite a state and started shouting at my guides. "Why aren't you guiding me?" "What do I have to do?" "Why am I here?" "I want to stay here, help me please, and guide me please" I was in a fair old state before I finally collapsed into bed.

Whatever had been blocking me came out that evening. I realised the next day that whilst I had been in Spain I hadn't really taken the time to look at and work on my problems. If I couldn't afford to stay in Spain then I would have to return to the UK and return back to my stonework but at least I had given it my best shot. I had tried, and was still trying my best but I actually felt as though a large weight had been lifted from me.

That next morning I got up, showered but feeling very, very hung over walked down to my local bar to get some breakfast. As I approached the bar I noticed a sign in the window, 'Business for Sale', work in the sun, two days a week. I called the number and it was Dave, remember the one in the wheel chair, one of the first people I had spoken to in Spain regarding my therapy work. I had only met him once and here we were talking about the business he had for sale. Again, I do not believe in coincidences, this had happened for a reason and I know my guides had led me there. Maybe that was the reason I had met him in the first instance. The business was a market stall selling very good quality Thai silk shirts and various styles of polo shirts. The market was held Wednesday and Sunday on a very large local market in Benidorm. Dave and his wife, Ellie, wanted to retire. They were selling the stock, there would be no charge for the business but it included a small van (which I named Sooty) the stall, plus lots of extras. Dave said he would be willing to stay on and show who ever bought the business, how to run the stall, order goods, etc. I had many meetings with them and went to watch the stall in action on four occasions. I also involved myself with the setting up and dismantling of the stall. I was interested and could see it being my way to stay in Spain. It would hopefully, give me the income to support my stay. I spoke in depth to Jaqui and we felt we should give it a go; but at a cost of 13.000 Euros.

It was my guides who had led me that morning and I trusted in them totally. Sometimes I challenged them, why they have given me a certain direction but if I didn't want to do it, I wouldn't. My free will again. Josh and Nahkoma are not just my guides; they had become a very close energy to me. It had taken me a few years to get here but it all happened that evening. Obviously, a lot more happened but I'm not going to write about it here because it's very personal to me and I don't want to share it with everyone. The blockage my guides helped me remove had opened up a new world of spirituality. It's fantastic and I'm now exploring it. Lessons to learn and so much to understand but I know they will guide me and teach me.

How to connect with your guide or guides

I am going to give you one way of connecting to your guide. There are many different ways to do this but you need to follow what you feel is right for you. I didn't carry out research for this book or use other people's ideas. I write through my own knowledge and years of experience and work carried out with hundreds of people. There are many books in the market place teaching how to get in contact with your guides, many, many good ones. My way is through imagery. I never profess to be an expert in any of the areas I teach but I do understand how to link into the universal energy, through the chakras and my guides. I give whatever they give me and in return I share it with you to try.

First of all, I am going to ask you to relax, take some deep breaths in through your nose and exhale through your mouth, allow your body to relax. Do this for about five minutes and try not to be disturbed by things such as the telephone, children, excessive noise, etc. Do it when you have time and nothing is pressing, (try this part with your eyes closed please). You don't have to keep your eyes closed after the relaxation exercise but use your imagination. Just let it happen and don't worry.

Now (with your eyes open), imagine your chakras, beginning with and including your heart chakra starting to open and glow brightly, from the heart chakra to the crown chakra, slowly opening. See them opening and really feel the expansion happening in your mind. See it in your mind's eye, feel and see a white shaft of light coming from the universe. The shaft of light is coming into the crown chakra and filling all the four chakras with white light of spirit and energy. Take your time and look at the visions coming through. Really feel you are there and let your imagination take over.

Now I want the first thought that comes into your mind; give me an instant reply. You won't even have to think about it because it will be the first word or words that come into your thoughts. Take a deep breath and exhale and allow things to happen:

What is your guide's name?

Is your guide male or female?

What is he or she wearing?

Where is he or she from?

Ask why they are here now in your thoughts and let the replies flow.

I have done this many times on the internet with people from all over the world and many have linked with their guide fairly quickly. Don't worry if it didn't happen for you this time, it will. Try again later, when you're in bed, or perhaps relaxing in a comfortable chair. Your guide will appear in your thoughts; you have only to ask. Once you have raised the vibration and opened the chakras the energy will come and you will get images via the universal and spiritual energy you are allowing into your mind and body. Remember, (this is very important), when you have finished the exercise always balance your chakras and reduce the energy in the four top chakras to become closed again. Use imagery to see the chakras now in perfect balance and closed down.

I often had up to thirty people in my internet room and it was amazing the names of guides they were typing onto the screen and the things they could see and feel after this exercise. One woman had tried many years to contact and imagine her guide. That evening she connected very strongly with 'her' and to this day still works with that guide. Connecting to your guide doesn't need to be at all complex. Take your time.

Once you feel, or see the imagery of your guide in your thoughts I suggest you thank them and ask them for direction in the future. If it happens, as it did for me images of your guide will come in on a regular basis but remember you may do it differently. The choice is yours to explore. Just enjoy it because there is no right and certainly no wrong way.

My wife connected to 'Tomaho' a young native female guide during a similar session and has been working with her ever since using this technique.

Many people have asked me how I see and feel things. The image of Josh and Nahkoma come into my mind very clearly but I don't hear them as in "normal sound" but I know what they are saying to me. I hear everything they say through my inner sound. As I work more and more with my guides the images I receive have become clearer and appear much quicker. It takes time to learn, develop and understand and this happens on each new spiritual pathway.

I will explain in a later chapter how I apply universal energy through my hands as I do my healing work.

Guides are an important part of spiritual work and spiritual development, (my feelings), but not everyone uses a guide, some use and work with Angels. Others may work in a totally different spiritual area. I can only tell you what has happened on my journey with spirit. You may be on a different pathway or theme completely.

I firmly believe that everyone's life has a theme, we follow that theme for particular lessons we need to learn and understand. But you can always choose free will and go in whatever direction you feel is right for you, that is of your choice.

A REASON, A SEASON, A LIFETIME.

People come into your life for a reason, a season; or a lifetime.

When you figure out which it is you will know exactly what to do.

When someone is in your life for a REASON, it is usually to meet a need you have expressed outwardly or inwardly.

They have come to assist you through a difficulty, to provide you with guidance and support, to aid you physically, emotionally, or spiritually.

They may seem like a Godsend, and they are.

They are there for the reason you need them to be there.

Then, without any wrongdoing on your part or at an inconvenient time, this person will say or do something to bring the relationship to an end.

Sometimes they die.

Sometimes they walk away.

Sometimes they act up or out and force you to take a stand.

What we must realise is that our need has been met, our desire fulfilled; their work is done.

The prayer you sent up has been answered and it is now time to move on.

When people come into your life for a SEASON, it is because your turn has come to share, grow, or learn.

They may bring you an experience of peace or make you laugh. They may teach you something you have never done.

They usually give you an unbelievable amount of joy.

Believe it! It is real! But only for a season.

LIFETIME relationships teach lifetime lessons. Those things you must build upon in order to have a solid emotional foundation.

Your job is to accept the lesson. Love the person/people (any way) and put what you have learned to use in all other relationships and areas of your life.

Author unknown

It is said that love is blind but friendship is clairvoyant.

8. Working With Your Inner Child

Over the years I have taught many people how to link to their inner child and get back in-touch with an area that has possibly been missing from their life for a long time. Again there is no right or wrong way

It is all to do with the way things are perceived in childhood and how it may have influenced the person in their adult life. Sometimes we lose that child within because we simply grow up and forget about the child within. Learning to become adult, with all the responsibility that goes with it; putting on the stiff upper lip. Many people try to work spiritually but if the inner child remains lost somewhere in the background, or at a distance, it becomes hard to grow. You have to learn to bring the child back to play in your life. Let the adult be involved in looking after you, whilst the child within brings in a balance of love, fun and energy for you to continue on your pathway. It's all about energy and your own internal balance.

In my sessions I relax my client into hypnosis and ask them to see a child standing about ten feet in front of them. The child has their back to them and the face cannot be seen. I usually ask if the child can be seen clearly and the reply is normally a very quick 'yes'. I then ask if the child is male or female most people give the same sex as themselves. I ask my client not move towards the child but to stay where they are until I suggest otherwise. I use this technique to begin to uncover any hidden repressions that may be inside, buried from childhood.

I ask for the child's name and usually it's the clients own name but occasionally I might be given a different name. It actually doesn't matter what name they give as long as they keep the image strongly in their mind. I then ask how the child feels, sometimes I get a very fast reaction, tears suddenly began to flow and this is the upset inner child. If this happens, I ask the child to turn round and ask the adult to gently ask the child what is wrong. Normally, a childhood issue will come out, a memory that has been upsetting the child subconsciously, for a long time.

When the child has finished speaking, I ask them to move a little closer to each other but not to touch. I normally ask what the adult would like to do and it's very usual for the adult to reply, "I just want to hug her/him". This is the point the energy to heal comes in. I suggest that they stand very close together, looking at each other. I then ask them both this question: "Are you ready to let go of anything, any memory from the past that may have upset you, confused you, scared you, made you angry, or hurt you in any way or form?" Once they have answered, I always ask the adult to let me know what the child said. I ask them to embrace each other and the adult to pull the child deep into the heart chakra and to let me know when they have achieved this.

Here are a few replies I have had from this kind of session, showing how well it can work when applied correctly. If you think about it, we are coming back to balance yet again; and it's all to do with balance, Yin Yang and energy. When I work with a person, one to one on the inner child, Nahkoma is with me very strongly and he guides me with that person's energy.

“Thank you for the facilitation and guidance through the inner child healing and also to the introduction to some of my past lives”.

“The inner child had excruciating pain and inhibited my heart chakra for ages, this dissolved leaving behind a complete sense of relief, joy and peace.”

“Thanks for the inner child healing today. It was so good to be integrated with the fun-loving child within! Seeing and feeling that little girl’s sorrow melt away, was one of the most moving moments I’ve ever experienced”.

I retain many; similar letters and emails from people but these are an example to show how effective it can be. It is very important in life to keep the balance between the adult and the child; balance and harmony intact. This in turn allows a well-balanced mind when it comes to working with energy or spirit.

I use many techniques when working in this direction but the one above is without doubt a very powerful tool. I do feel from what I have observed over the years it is important to clear some, if not all the debris from the subconscious. It is also good to have personal experience and to have an understanding of what others may experience. There are many ways of helping people and over the years I have met many wonderful people who help others in this direction. I applaud you all, without our teachers where would we be?

9. Healing & My Work With Spirit & Energy

I suppose I have been using healing in many ways for a long time in my hypnotherapy work but I had never been aware of it being spiritual, not until I started working with my guides and when I became more aware of auras and energy. I had been using energy through my hands to help remove headaches and help people to relax. I wasn't aware of what I was really doing and when I did the ego took over. I thought it was me doing these things rather than the spiritual energy coming through me. I was nothing more than a conduit of that energy. I wasn't aware in the early days that I was opening my chakras and connecting to the universal energy. I thought I had special powers, how wrong I was.

As my knowledge developed I became more aware of auras and the energy involved, especially when I started using the aura camera. It seemed as if all my knowledge over the years was coming together into a bigger picture. I could not only see the auras being projected onto the screen, I was beginning to sense them around people. I felt directions to particular areas of the aura, long before anyone sat down and went on the camera. I still don't see the auras like some people but I do sense them and the energy around someone and I can scan the body with my hands. I never do this without permission of course, not only would it be rude to do so, but it may make a person feel very ill at ease.

A venue in Manchester made me realise how strong energy could become.

I received a telephone call one evening, from a very large department store in Manchester and was asked if I could attend the launch of a new product. They wanted me to demonstrate my aura camera to the guests.

I didn't have to produce any printouts, just allow people to sit and see their auras live and explain the colours to individuals. I agreed to go and on the given date duly arrived at the rear of the store at 9 p.m. as agreed. I was to be ready at approximately 10 p.m. Security was very tight so I assumed there were some very important and influential people inside.

I was escorted upstairs by a security guard and shown where to set up. I could hear the music in the adjoining room and could see some of the demonstrations taking place. The place was packed with people eating, partaking of a few glasses of wine and enjoying the entertainment.

A short time later I heard the compere speak about the aura camera and tell the guests where they could find me after the show.

The entertainment ended and it was like a stampede, people coming from everywhere but they soon formed an orderly line. Some were a bit giggly, possibly, after a little too much red wine. In turn, they sat down with me and I took them through the programme. I was extremely drawn to one woman and in particular to her neck and shoulder area; just as I have done with so many others. As she went on the camera the image on the screen showed the areas I had linked to. I asked her if I could use my hand to remove some of the blocked energy I could feel. It was at that point she told me about her 'frozen shoulder' which she'd had for many years. I linked to my guides and drew down the energy and put my hand behind her neck, possibly about two feet away from her body. Instantly there was massive surge of energy through my hand and beads of sweat appeared very suddenly on the front of her chest and forehead. I quickly pulled my hand away from her. She had felt the surge of energy and she was now shaking. I apologised to her but must admit I was somewhat stunned as to what had just taken place. She stood up, turned around and quite bewildered said, "Look, I can move my arm". How did you do that?

Whatever happened certainly worked that evening and it was meant to be. But it taught me a valuable lesson. Sometimes I have to increase the energy slowly and not just dive straight in, 'all guns blazing'. I received a lovely thank you call from the event organisers a few days later. I enquired about the lady guest's shoulder and was told it was fine. She and her friends were still trying to fathom out how I had done it. When working with energy you need to be very aware of what you're doing. Since that evening I always make sure I bring the energy in slowly, making sure my client is comfortable before increasing the energy level.

When I first began healing and working with energy I used to cup my hands. I would imagine a white ball of energy in them and visualise a white shaft of light coming into them directly from the universe. The heat would start to build up in my hands until I felt it was strong enough to use in my healing. I would then enter the person's aura, with permission of course and place my hand or hands over the affected areas and wait until the person could feel the energy entering their body. I then brought the energy down into the person's body through touch. Through thought and my own imagery I projected the energy into the area where it was needed. At that point I would remove my hands pulling any negative energy into my hands. I always released the energy I took and sent it up into the universe for disposal. I then washed my hands with water to neutralise the effect.

That is how I began healing but since then many things have changed in the way I work with spirit and energy.

I will now explain how Josh gave me shields in my wrists.

One evening, whilst listening on the internet to people discussing about spiritual protection, I became aware of people becoming ill after a period of time when working with energy and healing. It made me wonder if they were taking on the other person's energy. I asked Josh for guidance and that is when he came and placed spiritual shields in my wrists. The shields would never allow any negative energy through my wrists into my body. Josh brought them in very fast, it actually happened whilst I was sat having my evening meal. The energy was very strong and the imagery Josh brought with him was very clear. I actually saw them being placed in my wrists. A very strange thing to happen whilst you're eating but that is exactly how it happened. Even now, as I'm typing this, I am still aware of the shields.

When I'm working with someone I get imagery of the inside of that person. Over the years, my healing, for some reason draws more and more to necks, shoulders, backs and spinal areas. The aura camera usually confirms this. It has become a really good partnership, working with the aura camera and my guides.

I could now use my hands and scan the aura, feeling for the colder areas or different sensations. I then move my hand closer until I get a feeling of what's happening inside that person. I touch them, (with prior consent), my guides are with me, assisting all the time. I usually get dark or grey images in my imagery. I am usually given an image of any internal problems, and how that person feels, (Empathic). I always go with what I'm told and focus on that image. Once, when working with one person who had been having trouble with her shoulder I could see white doves coming into the area. They were taking away the greyness and making the entire energy perfect in a brilliant white light. I often get white doves coming in now, along with white butterflies and white ribbons of light.

Sometimes through my guides I get white light into my fingers. I inject the white healing energy and light into the affected area through my fingers, just like a hypodermic syringe. My imagery is different with each person but I can usually sense when I've got hold of the negative area and pull it into my hands to be disposed of by spirit later. Remember it cannot enter my body because of the shields in my wrists.

Recently, I have been asking people to concentrate their thoughts on the area just below the navel and when I count to three, to push the negative energy from that area into my hands. I've seen people nearly fall off their seats doing this but it works. I always make sure they are sitting because once I nearly had man fall over; lesson learned.

Whilst I was living in Spain, a neighbour, who knew a little bit about my work, came to me and asked if I could do my 'Hocus Pocus' on her back. She had been suffering for a number of weeks with acute pain. Within ten minutes of working with her she could move easily, free of pain. She could even bend and touch the floor and the pain never returned.

As I've continued developing my healing work I have noticed that the energy comes when I ask for it. It appears automatically but prior to any healing session I always ask for permission. I call my guides and ask spirit for the connection to the universal energy before working with anyone. After I have finished I always give grateful thanks to all involved through a silent prayer.

I feel that everyone has the ability to heal others and I hope I've given you some insight on healing. Try for yourself, place your hands over someone's aura, about two inches from the skin and then begin sensing what you feel, close your eyes if it helps. You may feel coldness at times or a very strong heat, don't be amazed if the person you're with feels the heat from your hands, or the energy transmitted but please always ask for permission first.

Use your imagination when working with headaches, see the image you've been given. How does the person 'see' the headache, maybe red or angry? It is essential you see that imagery in your mind before placing your hand over their brow or before sending in a white, shining, healing light. This will come through you; a shaft of light, from the universe to overpower and take away the headache. As you take away your hand all the red or anger will be removed, leaving the white light of spirit behind. After a session always wash your hands to neutralise the energy.

Over the years I have gone on my own instinct and my guide's direction but I am going to say it again and no doubt I will keep reminding you. This is me, not you and I walk my pathway just as you will walk yours. You may work in a totally different way to others but it doesn't matter, go in the direction that you feel is right for you and use what you feel deep inside and work with it. I'm not here to question anyone else's work and say that my way is the right way; that would be egoism, (long gone). As I told you at the beginning, I was brought up without any religion but I do believe in God (my God) and it works fine for me.

Energy Ball and Distant Healing

I have used this technique many times over the years and find it a very powerful way of creating energy. This technique can also be used for sending the energy you have created to someone who could be thousands of miles away and who may be in need of healing.

Firstly, sit in a relaxed upright position where you're not going to be interrupted for a while. Clear your thoughts and imagine that you can see and feel a round ball of energy inside your cupped hands. See it as an image of Earth, as it would be seen from outer space; see it clearly in your mind's eye between your cupped hands. Imagine that you're feeling it vibrate and that you are connecting to the Earth's vibrations with your own vibrations. You may feel a form of energy starting and coming into your hands. I feel it getting slightly warmer and starting to vibrate more.

When you can see this image clearly and start to feel any form of energy coming into your hands ask for the scene to change. Let the image of the Earth disappear and replace it with a' white ball' of pure energy. When I'm doing this I see a sparkly round ball of white light and energy. Ask it and allow it to grow in energy.

Once this image is clear and you can see and feel its vibrations I would like you to imagine, a narrow beam of white light coming down from the universe and entering your energy ball and as it does it increases in energy. Ask for Universal energy to assist you in your energy or healing work, allowing it to happen in your mind's eye.

See in your mind the person you want to send the healing energy to. Picture them as clearly as you can and bring a beam of white light from your energy ball between your hands and direct it towards them. Cover them in pure white healing energy. Light comes down from the Universe into your energy ball and a beam of light and healing energy is then directed to the person.

There is no right or wrong way but I do know through personal experience that energy and healing can be sent anywhere, distance is no object.

Over the years I have become very proficient and can draw in universal energy very quickly and send it in a blink of an eye. I have learned how to direct the energy, once it has built up between my hands, to simply go where I feel the affected area is and release the energy into it.

A very high percentage would go to the exact place and the person would feel a warmth or tingling sensation. Of course I wasn't very adept when I first started using this universal energy but after years of practice it has become much faster and clearer. I trust in it totally now.

10. Twelve Things You Were Not Taught In School About Creative Thinking

1. You are creative.

The artist is not a special person, each one of us is a special kind of artist. Every one of us is born a creative, spontaneous thinker. The only difference between the people who are creative and the ones who are not, is a simple belief. Creative people believe they are creative. People, who believe they are not creative, are not. Once you have a particular identity and set of beliefs about yourself you become interested in seeking out the skills needed to express your identity and beliefs. This is why people who believe they are creative become creative. If you believe you are not creative, then there is no need to learn how to become creative and you don't. The reality is that believing you are not creative excuses you from trying or attempting anything new. When someone tells you that they are not creative you are talking to someone who has no interest and will make no effort to be a creative thinker.

2. Creative thinking is work.

You must have passion and the determination to immerse yourself in the process of creating new and different ideas. You must then have patience to persevere against all adversity. All creative geniuses work passionately hard and produce incredible numbers of ideas, most of which are bad. In fact, more bad poems were written by the major poets than by minor poets. Thomas Edison created 3000 different ideas for lighting systems before he evaluated them for practicality and profitability. Wolfgang Amadeus Mozart produced more than six hundred pieces of music, including forty-one symphonies and some forty-odd operas and masses, during his short creative life. Rembrandt produced around 650 paintings and 2,000 drawings and Picasso executed more than 20,000 works. Shakespeare wrote 154 sonnets. Some were masterpieces, while others were no better than his contemporaries could have written and some were simply bad.

3. You must go through the motions of being creative.

When you are producing ideas, you are replenishing neurotransmitters linked to genes which are being turned on and off in response to what your brain is doing, which in turn responds to challenges. When you go through the motions of trying to come up with new ideas, you are energizing your brain by increasing the number of contacts between neurons. The more times you try to get ideas, the more active your brain becomes and the more creative you become. If you want to become an artist and all you did was paint a picture every day, you will become an artist. You may not become another Vincent Van Gogh but you will become more of an artist than someone who has never tried.

4. Your brain is not a computer.

Your brain is a dynamic system that evolves its patterns of activity rather than computes them like a computer. It thrives on the creative energy of feedback from experiences real or fictional. You can synthesise experience, literally create it in your own imagination. The human brain cannot tell the difference between an "actual" experience and an experience imagined vividly and in detail. This discovery is what enabled Albert Einstein to create his thought experiments with imaginary scenarios which led to his revolutionary ideas about space and time. One day, for example, he imagined falling in love. Then he imagined meeting the woman he fell in love with, two weeks later he fell in love. This led to his theory of causality. The same process of synthesising experience allowed Walt Disney to bring his fantasies to life.

5. There is no one right answer.

Reality is ambiguous. Aristotle said, "It is either A or not-A". It cannot be both. The sky is either blue or not blue. This is black and white thinking as the sky is a billion different shades of blue. A beam of light is either a wave or not a wave (A or not-A). Physicists discovered that light can be either a wave or particle depending on the viewpoint of the observer. The only certainty in life is uncertainty. When trying to get ideas, do not censor or evaluate them as they occur. Nothing kills creativity faster than self-censorship of ideas while generating them. Think of all your ideas as possibilities and generate as many as you can before you decide which ones to select. The world is not black or white. It is grey.

6. Never stop with your first good idea

Always strive to find a better one and continue until you have one that is still better. In 1862, Phillip Reis demonstrated his invention which could transmit music over the wires. He was days away from improving it into a telephone that could transmit speech. Every communication expert in Germany dissuaded him from making improvements, as they said the telegraph is good enough. No one would buy or use a telephone. Ten years later, Alexander Graham Bell patented the telephone. Spencer Silver developed a new adhesive for 3M that stuck to objects but could easily be lifted off. It was first marketed as a bulletin board adhesive so the boards could be moved easily from place to place. There was no market for it. Silver didn't discard it. One day Arthur Fry, another 3M employee, was singing in the church's choir when his page marker fell out of his hymnal. Fry coated his page markers with Silver's adhesive and discovered the markers stayed in place, yet lifted off without damaging the page. Hence the Post-it Notes were born. Thomas Edison was always trying to spring board from one idea to another in his work. He spring boarded his work from the telephone (sounds transmitted) to the phonograph (sounds recorded) and finally, to motion pictures (images recorded).

7. Expect the experts to be negative.

The more expert and specialised a person becomes, the more their mind set becomes narrowed and the more fixated they become on confirming what they believe to be absolute. Consequently, when confronted with new and different ideas, their focus will be on conformity. Does it conform to what I know is right? If not, experts will spend all their time showing and explaining why it can't be done and why it can't work. They will not look for ways to make it work, or get it done because this might demonstrate that what they regarded as absolute is not absolute at all. This is why when Fred Smith created Federal Express; every delivery expert in the U.S. predicted its certain doom. After all, they said, "If this delivery concept was doable, the Post Office or UPS would have done it long ago."

8. Trust your instincts.

Don't allow yourself to get discouraged. Albert Einstein was expelled from school because his attitude had a negative effect on serious students. He failed his university entrance exam and had to attend a trade school for one year before finally being admitted. He was the only one in his graduating class who did not get a teaching position because no professor would recommend him. One professor said Einstein was "the laziest dog" the university ever had. Beethoven's parents were told he was too stupid to be a music composer. Charles Darwin's colleagues called him a fool, doing "fool's experiments" when he worked on his theory of biological evolution. Walt Disney was fired from his first job on a newspaper because "he lacked imagination." Thomas Edison had only two years of formal schooling, was totally deaf in one ear and was hard of hearing in the other. He was fired from his first job as a newsboy and later fired from his job as a telegrapher and still he became the most famous inventor in the history of the U.S.

9. There is no such thing as failure.

Whenever you try to do something and do not succeed, you do not fail. You have learned something that does not work. Always ask "What have I learned about what doesn't work?", "Can this explain something that I didn't set out to explain?", and "What have I discovered that I didn't set out to discover?" Whenever someone tells you that they have never made a mistake, you are talking to someone who has never tried anything new.

10. You do not see things as they are; you see them as you are.

Interpret your own experiences. All experiences are neutral. They have no meaning. You give them meaning by the way you choose to interpret them. If you are a priest, you see evidence of God everywhere. If you are an atheist, you see the absence of God everywhere. IBM observed that no one in the world had a personal computer. IBM interpreted this to mean there was no market. College dropouts, Bill Gates and Steve Jobs, looked at the same absence of personal computers and saw a massive opportunity. Once, Thomas Edison was approached by an assistant while working on the filament for the light bulb. The assistant asked Edison why he didn't give up. "After all," he said, "you have failed 5000 times." Edison looked at him and told him that he didn't understand what the assistant meant by failure, because, Edison said, "I have discovered 5000 things that don't work." You construct your own reality by how you choose to interpret your experiences.

11. Always approach a problem on its own terms.

Do not trust your first perspective of a problem as it will be too biased toward your usual way of thinking. Always look at your problem from multiple perspectives. Always remember that genius is finding a perspective no one else has taken. Look for different ways to look at the problem. Write the problem statement several times using different words. Take another role, for example, how would someone else see it, how would Jay Leno, Pablo Picasso, George Patton see it? Draw a picture of the problem, make a model, or mold a sculpture. Take a walk and look for things that metaphorically represent the problem and force connections between those things and the problem (How is a broken store window like my communications problem with my students?) Ask your friends and strangers how they see the problem. Ask a child. How would a ten year old solve it? Ask a grandparent. Imagine you are the problem. When you change the way you look at things, the things you look at change.

12. Learn to think unconventionally.

Creative geniuses do not think analytically and logically. Conventional, logical, analytical thinkers are exclusive thinkers which mean they exclude all information that is not related to the problem. They look for ways to eliminate possibilities. Creative geniuses are inclusive thinkers which mean they look for ways to include everything, including things that are dissimilar and totally unrelated. Generating associations and connections between unrelated or dissimilar subjects is how they provoke different thinking patterns in their brain. These new patterns lead to new connections which give them a different way to focus on the information and different ways to interpret what they are focusing on. This is how original and truly novel ideas are created. Albert Einstein once famously remarked *"Imagination is more important than knowledge. For knowledge is limited to all we now know and understand, while imagination embraces the entire world and all there ever will be to know and understand."*

And, finally, creativity is paradoxical. To create, a person must have knowledge but forget the knowledge, must see unexpected connections in things but not have a mental disorder, must work hard but spend time doing nothing as information incubates, must create many ideas yet most of them are useless, must look at the same thing as everyone else, yet see something different, must desire success but embrace failure, must be persistent but not stubborn, and must listen to experts but know how to disregard them.

Michael Michalko is the author of the highly acclaimed Thinkertoys: A Handbook of Creative Thinking Techniques. His newest book Creative Thinkering: Putting your Imagination to Work has just been released and is now available at most major bookstores.

Here are 25 life lessons from Albert Einstein:

1. Intellectual growth should commence at birth and cease only at death.

2. Everyone should be respected as an individual, but no one idolized.

3. Never do anything against conscience even if the state demands it.

4. If people are good only because they fear punishment, and hope for reward, then we are a sorry lot indeed.

5. A perfection of means, and confusion of aims, seems to be our main problem.

6. Love is a better teacher than duty.

7. If you can't explain it simply, you don't understand it well enough.

8. No problem can be solved from the same level of consciousness that created it.

9. Insanity: doing the same thing over and over again and expecting different results.

10. Learn from yesterday, live for today, hope for tomorrow.

11. It has become appallingly obvious that our technology has exceeded our humanity.

12. Everything that can be counted does not necessarily count; everything that counts cannot necessarily be counted.

13. Force always attracts men of low morality.

14. Everything should be as simple as it is, but not simpler.

15. A man should look for what is, and not for what he thinks should be.

16. Any man who reads too much and uses his own brain too little falls into lazy habits of thinking.

17. A person who never made a mistake, never tried anything new.

18. It is the supreme art of the teacher to awaken joy in creative expression and knowledge.

19. Anyone who doesn't take truth seriously in small matters cannot be trusted in large ones either.

20. Great spirits have always encountered violent opposition from mediocre minds.

21. Education is what remains after one has forgotten what one has learned in school.

22. Logic will get you from A to B. Imagination will take you everywhere.

23. Anger dwells only in the bosom of fools.

24. Information is not knowledge.

25. Never lose a holy curiosity.

Even the smartest people out there sometimes forget some of those obvious concepts:

Not feeling ready can be a good thing

Opportunities rarely come when we are 100% ready to seize them. They are more likely to knock on your door when you feel insecure with your preparation, knowledge and skills. But that doesn't mean you should be ignoring them until you feel ready. Most of our lifetime opportunities force us to grow both emotionally and intellectually. They push us to give the best of ourselves, even if that means getting out of our comfort zones. But sacrificing our comfort can give us the chance for personal growth. If you want to change your life for the better, you should open yourself to the opportunities that arise, even if you don't feel 100% ready.

Success and failure go hand in hand

Often time's people tend to misinterpret the meaning of the word "failure". Why are we so afraid of failure? It is just as natural as succeeding. Failure doesn't mean not succeeding. It is actually a part of the circle of success. And success itself shouldn't be measured by the achievement of a particular goal.

Success is a state of being and therefore, everyone can feel successful.

Action is the key for all success

We often hear that knowledge is power. But it only is power if you use it. Knowing how to do something and actually doing it are two completely different things. It doesn't matter if, for example, you read books and articles on fighting procrastination, and take no particular action to overcome that problem. Knowledge and intelligence are useless without action.

Even mistakes mean progress

If you look back in your life, maybe you will realise that the mistakes you have made in the past have taught you valuable lessons. So why should we be scared of making mistakes, if they help us grow stronger and wiser? Every mistake you make on the way to a particular goal brings you one step closer to achieving it. It is highly possible that the mistake you will regret the most in your life is not taking action because of the fear of making mistakes. This way you will always be wondering what could have happened, if you hadn't been so scared. And most importantly-you wouldn't have made any progress. So don't be afraid of feeling uncertain about something- give it a try and see what happens.

Making decisions is impeded when there are too many options
We live in times when there are so many opportunities for us to choose from when it comes to determining our career and life paths. But when we have so many choices before us, we can often at times get confused and indecisive. Business and

marketing studies prove that when a consumer has more product choices, he's predisposed to buy less. If you think about it, choosing one product out of three product choices feels much easier than choosing one out of three hundred. Most people will give up easily, if the buying decision process is tough.

Success doesn't necessarily mean happiness

Many people believe that they can only be happy if they accomplish a particular goal. In my opinion, we can choose to be happy every day, no matter where on the path to our goals we are at the moment. "The monk who sold his Ferrari" by Robin Sharma is one of the most inspiring books I have ever read. One of the main ideas shared by the author is that you don't have to wait to accomplish your dreams to be happy. The main character was one of the most successful lawyers in the country but even though he had everything he ever wanted, he wasn't a happy person. The most important thing is to cherish every moment of every day and to be thankful for who you are and what you have now.

You can be the best at something, even if you don't like doing it Some people say that in order to be good at doing something, you should love doing this thing. In my opinion, this isn't necessarily true. If a person devotes their time and effort to learn a particular skill, they can become excellent at it. How they feel about the activity doesn't determine their success in it.

What we see in others exists in us

When we have a problem with someone, this can actually help us learn more about ourselves. It can help us learn why we see that problem in the other person and the reason can be that we hold it inside of us also and seeing it exposed before us can be frustrating. But acknowledging that what we see in others is a reflection of ourselves can help us overcome our unsolved issues.

To experience the full spectrum of life, to taste all of the apples, we have to face our fears.

Fear is an emotion that we're all familiar with. For some of us, it's a constant companion, creeping around every corner we turn. While it can save us from entering a dangerous situation on the one hand, it can prevent us from pursuing a life changing opportunity on the other. Fear can keep us from applying for our dream job, boarding an airplane, falling in love and worst of all, from fulfilling our true and highest purpose. One thing is for certain, the more power we give fear, the more it lords over us, calling all the shots and robbing us of peace.

But facing our fears is the quickest way to squelch them. And sometimes in life, that which we fear most happens. Regardless of whether we want to face these fears, we have to. Here I list 10 fears that you'll inevitably have to face (some you likely already have) and explain to you why you are better equipped and more fearless than you may now believe.

1. You will lose someone you can't live without. And it will feel as though your world is crashing down on top of you. You

will wonder how you can possibly go on. And the bad news is you won't really. Not that version of you anyhow. When you lose someone who means the world to you, you never really get over that loss. But this is also the good news. They live forever in your shattered heart. And one day, you realize that it is the very holes and cracks they've left you with, that allow your light to shine through.

2. You will be utterly and completely alone. For the first part of our lives, most of us are seduced by the idea that we are not alone because there are people all around us. But some time in your late twenties or early thirties the reality hits you: you're completely and utterly alone. Unlike childhood, when everyone appears to be revolving their lives around you, adulthood proves that everyone is looking out for their own best interest. And you have to do the same. At once, you feel the sting of loneliness and the freedom of solitude. In general, aloneness seems to be feared and avoided; yet every great spiritual teacher has attested to its importance. And the true beauty is that we're all alone in our aloneness. Once we can grasp this concept, we may just find that life's not so lonely after all.

3. Be betrayed by someone close to you. People will disappoint you. Everyone suffers at least one bad betrayal in their lifetime. It's part of what unites us. But the trick is to not let that experience destroy our trust in people. We can't let them take that from us, too. People will always be our greatest assets and our greatest liabilities. The great challenge is to keep caring for them no matter what.

4. Give up a dream. When we're young, the world is our playground and the sky is the limit. We come out of education

wanting to change the world, to get married, and have kids. But we get into the middle and discover it's harder than we thought. People move away, addictions are formed, and opportunities are lost. And amidst it all, we change. For most of us, that means our dreams change too. It can be one of the hardest and scariest things in the world to give up on a dream. Though, perhaps we should re-frame this notion as not one of giving up but of letting go. Letting go of an idea that you've held of how your life would be by this point in time, and embracing with gratitude all that your life is.

5. Lose total control. The truth is most of our lives are out of our control. Yet somehow, the majority of us live with this sort of mirage that we are behind the steering wheel. We make plans and then feel disappointed when they don't happen. We expect things from people that they don't do or can't give. No matter how hard we try, we simply can't control everything. At some point, it hits us all, a period of complete and total loss of control. Like a fast, downward spiral-shaped roller coaster that you can't remember ever boarding. It's scary but it happens to all of us. And it's our choice whether we scream with terror or simply let go to appreciate the ride, or both.

6. You'll screw up. You'll hurt someone you never meant to. You'll fail a test you thought you'd pass. You'll forget to send that all-important email that you promised to your friend. Stuff happens. And you're not perfect. None of us are. We have to accept the fact that we're going to make mistakes. And we have to forgive ourselves when we do. It is only when we stop expecting ourselves and others to be perfect, that we can love everyone for who they are.

7. You'll fail. If screwing up is scary, than failing is terrifying. But perhaps a more accurate depiction of this fear is that we lose. On top of our own internal and deeply rooted competitive drive, our culture is so win, win, win, that when we do lose, we feel like we've failed. But how terribly wrong we are! A loss is not a failure. A loss means you've tried for something! Sadly, some people are so scared of failing that they instead choose to not try at all. But if we don't take risks, then we can't succeed. And the only true failure is not trying. Besides, when you lose, scary as it might seem, you find another part of yourself.

8. Suffer a crushing heartbreak. This fear encompasses and yet at the same time is distinct from all the others on this list. For example, if you're going through a heart-wrenching breakup, in many ways, you're facing a death and failure; the death and failure of that relationship. Yet again, this is something we all must go through. In order to find ourselves, we must first lose ourselves. It takes a heart that's been broken, to experience real compassion. And although in the wake of heart break, it may feel like we're standing deep in a forest with no way out, we can find hope in the knowledge that someone else has stood in our exact spot, and has since moved on.

9. You'll disappoint people. And likely face a lot of criticism on the way. I think it's our nature to want to please. As children, we learn our worth by seeing how often (or not) we can please those around us. But as the years pass and we begin to pursue our own goals and plans, we learn that we can't please everybody. We disappoint people on a regular basis and if we're truly doing something extraordinary, then we face a lot of criticism along the way. But take it from Donald Rumsfeld

who said it best, "If you are not criticised, you may not be doing much."

10. Life will throw a wrench in your plans. They say if you want to hear God laugh, tell him your plans. And it's true. No matter how immaculate your organisation or detailed your schemes, things usually won't go as you expect. There is only so much for which we can plan. So we take life as it comes, one day at a time, with hope. We remain as prepared and proactive as we can, then relinquish our control. In this life, the only thing we should ever be expecting is the unexpected.

Congratulations. If you've already faced a number of the fears on this list, than you are ahead of the game. You've experienced the lows of life and you've come out on top. You're living life to the fullest, though it may not always feel that way. You're skating across the peaks, and trudging on through the valleys. It's what life is all about! And for this, you're braver than you believe and stronger than you think. Your character runs deep and you are better equipped than most to handle life's continued challenges. Be grateful for your hardships that have made you who you are today.

In the words of Marianne Williamson, *"Love is what we were born with. Fear is what we learned here."* Fears cease to be fears once we face them. Even if we don't want to face them, often we have no choice. But the key, I've learned, to facing trials and tribulations, is managing to come out on top, is acceptance and faith. Accepting our reality at any given moment, no matter how scary it may seem and having faith in ourselves and others. The reality is that difficulties seldom defeat people but lack of faith in themselves usually does. Ultimately, faith is what gives us the courage to face our fears, knowing in the end, and no matter what, we will be okay.

About this Author..

This article was written by Whitney Anthony. Whitney, loves singing, writing, and performing and is the author of the Vehicle of Wisdom blog. Although she has graduated from school, Whitney considers herself a lifelong student. She believes that as we learn, we teach – at our best we are all teachers. To learn more about Whitney visit her website

This is quite a lot to absorb but well worth rereading many times. And does it make sense? Of course it does, try it for yourselves and see where it leads you. See what answers come up within your own mind and thoughts.

I know many people will be able to relate to the points below and I myself have and still do experience these 'truths' about not succeeding my dreams or goals. Many of these truths are obvious but many people do not accept or realise that they do them on a regular basis and blame other forces for their unsatisfied lives. I hope though that having more awareness as to why your situation in life is not what you want it to be helps in your pursuit of your dreams. There is no ultimate truth as to why you are here and no one thing that will fill that hole, though many people find some comfort in feeling that that ultimate truth can be an invisible force that's within and around you at all times at every moment of your life. For some, that realisation is all they need for well – happiness.

Based on your religious, political or ethical background you may already have an idea of what your dream is. Though I write this post with the intention of displaying the obvious truths the common, everyday working person faces in their pursuit of happiness. In our deranged politically and economically controlled society people often find themselves in a situation where they ponder the notion of dropping everything and following their dreams. Most people are tied down by jobs and money to simply drop everything though there is always time to work on your dream even if it's only a few moments of your day spent working on it – it adds up!

It's time to do some reevaluating of your life and really find out what it is you want to do. I myself am still on this seemingly endless search though I feel I will get there. It may seem prejudiced writing this article without living my own dream, though I see these as obvious truths we all choose to ignore and suppress in our daily lives but we all still wonder why, "I am not living the life I want to live."

"When was it when you stopped dreaming and became a man?"

1. You are all thought and no action

By this I mean you are a day dreamer, you ponder great ideas and fantasies but never act or attempt to pursue and satisfy these abstract interests. You lay in bed every night wishing you had worked on that project today or elaborated on that idea, eagerly waiting for tomorrow so you can finally attempt to put your dream in motion. You are never going to achieve anything or any dream for that matter without some practical effort involved. Try carrying around a notebook and pen for when inspiration arises and act on the ideas you have as soon as possible before you have time to second guess your thoughts.

2. You take every opportunity you can to slack off

You sleep in, take long showers, take an unnecessarily long time to do simple tasks, watch too much television, spend too much time on your phone and use those spare seconds in your day to stare of blankly waiting for time to pass by. What are you waiting for? To get home so you can do nothing and then do the same the next day? Seems like you are just waiting for retirement where you will have all the time in the world to ponder the things you wish you had of done in the earlier years of your life. Why not just push yourself while you are still resilient and pursue something you really want to do, what's the worst that can happen? Even if you get there and it's not what you expected the world is your oyster and the next opportunity is waiting around the corner if you are willing to take that next step yourself!

3. Your downtime is unproductive

This kind of relates to number 3, though I felt like separating it for one reason or another. If you were to calculate time you could have otherwise spent being productive i.e. downtime, you would most likely have months maybe years' worth of more well spent time working towards or doing something you love. If you were to use all that that downtime in a productive manner such as maybe reading, writing or planning your goals and dreams you would most likely find yourself in a situation where you are more flexible with what path you want to take in life. Finding some habits to get into that either help your thinking or work towards some form of goal may be worthwhile looking in to so you can stop wasting time and actually do something you want to do.

4. You neglect you!

No, I am not talking about physical and mental health (but that does matter). What I mean by neglecting yourself is that you suppress what makes you a conscious human. Without sounding too much like a mystic, you neglect your subconscious desire for intuition and change which is what makes you, you. Ideas and thoughts are suppressed either because you believe that are impractical or your firm morals and conservative beliefs stop any kind of development. We as humans strive for change and seeking of the unknown, so what is stopping you from branching out and doing something a little different, drop the 'if only' and pick up 'what-if'. Ever feel like your ideas or dreams won't work? Have a quick look around the internet and you will find loads of ideas and people who are well on the weird side but are making it big and living their dreams.

5. Lastly, maybe you just do not have dreams….

If you think these tips are silly and that the orthodox, conservative routine you live day to day is the only way to live, than your mindset is most of the problem. The only way to live a dream is firstly, to have a dream. You would be surprised at the amount of people who do not really have a desired dream that they could openly discuss when asked the question 'What is your dream?' Many would say money, a solid job or family but they are only key roles that are played in your dreams, overall production and not the dream itself. You need to really ask yourself, when I'm dead, will I have lived the life I really wanted to live or the life others expected of me?

11. What is a Lost Soul?

Lost souls are people who are spiritually adrift. For whatever reason, these individuals have blocked the intuitive guidance coming from their higher selves. In doing this, they have also cut themselves off from feeling the infinite love of the universe and this leads to struggle, anger and sadness. As a result, a lost soul's life is very challenging. If you are currently working to raise your vibration and follow your highest path, you probably find it difficult to interact with lost souls. These individuals can be some of the most frustrating people to deal with because they radiate lower vibrational energy and the way that they interact with others can be quite off-putting. However, if we want to help these people we must react with sympathy, rather than anger and hostility. Lost souls need unconditional love more than the rest of us because they are so starved for it. Although this may be challenging at times, love and acceptance are really the only things we can give to help others who have lost their way. So, here are some of the frustrating symptoms of a lost soul and how best for us to react in order to help them:

1. Defensiveness: a lost soul is someone who is operating from their ego, not from their higher self. Because they are largely ego-driven, lost souls will often feel the need to defend their positions and assert that they are always right, and always know best. Even friendly advice that will genuinely help a lost soul is often immediately discarded with a "Yeah, but…" followed by a list of reasons why they believe the advice won't work for them; your best reaction to this defensiveness?

Accept it. Do not engage in an argument with a lost soul, even if you feel like your advice is exactly what they need. Remember, lost souls are blocking their inner guidance, so they will very likely block beneficial advice from wherever it is coming from. The best you can do is put your ideas on the table, but then back away from the discussion when they push against it. Surprisingly, when I have done this in the past I have noticed that many such individuals will later tell me "I remember when you told me such-and-such, that was really good advice!" The thing about lost souls is that they do not like to have their egos challenged, so if you do not debate against their rebuttals they are far more likely to listen to your well-intended advice because they didn't feel threatened by your approach.

2. Closed-mindedness: Many times lost souls will not be interested in accepting different people and different choices. Again, the higher self is all-loving and all-accepting. If someone is blocking the unconditional love from their higher self they will be unable to radiate unconditional love to others. As a result, their "love" will only be given out to certain people who are behaving in a way that their ego approves of. Because of this, you will often see lost souls manifest themselves into people who are intolerant of other religions, bigoted, racist, homophobic or misogynistic. What would be your best reaction? If you feel as if something a lost soul tells you is intolerant or abusive towards others, very kindly tell them that it bothers you when they say things like that and then drop it. Remember, arguing with a lost soul is always a waste of time. Speak your mind and then move on. If you do not challenge a lost soul's ego, you will have the best shot at being heard.

3. Repeating the same mistakes, over and over again: (programmed) It may take many of us a few tries to learn a lesson in life but with a lost soul the pattern endlessly repeats itself. Later in this book I will show you a way how to change that patterning and belief via Pstec. You may often see a lost soul hopping from one abusive relationship to another, chronically being broke and out of work or even repeatedly being arrested and incarcerated. To be clear, none of us are perfect, and we're all making mistakes in some way. However, a lost soul's repeated mistakes are very painful and can cause them a lifetime of personal grief. What would be your reaction? Realise yet again, that a lost soul has severed ties with the love of the universe, therefore they do not understand how to make choices based on self-love. A lost soul has forgotten how to care for him or her. These individuals are not making their life decisions because they are trying to hurt themselves or anyone else, but rather because they have become blind to the guidance of the universe. In fact, quite often they make poor choices because they are simply trying to distract themselves or numb the pain of the emptiness they feel from being spiritually disconnected. Please do not judge them, do not chastise them and do not belittle their struggles. Accept them where they are, and love them anyway. This doesn't mean that you should allow them to pull you into their chaotic storms but do let them know that you care about them and you want the very best for them. Loving them from afar still counts! It can indeed be very frustrating to deal with a lost soul. The defensiveness, close-mindedness, and continuous self-harm can be very unpleasant to witness and interact with. That being said, it's good to remember that we are all on our own paths and we each have the option of travelling through life in the way that we choose. Although we may have found a higher calling, the lost souls are choosing to experience life in a limited way and that's their choice. Not one of us would want to be forced to think or believe something against our will and if we want the freedom of choice for ourselves we must allow the freedom of choice in others, even when we feel their choices are damaging and hurtful. We can speak our truths but we shouldn't feel the need to take on the job of changing the thoughts, beliefs and actions of others. At the end of the day, all we can really do for the lost souls of the world is accept and love them as they are, while being as happy, healthy and prosperous as we can be. If we can shine brightly enough, we just might provide enough light to help a lost soul find its way back.

What is Reiki Healing?

REIKI pronounced Ray-key is a natural method of healing on the universal life force.

REIKI is a technique founded by the Japanese for reducing stress and helping with relaxation while promoting healing. Reiki is administered by "laying on hands" and is founded on the belief that an unseen "life force energy" flows through every person and is what causes people to be alive. If one's "life force energy" gets too low, they are more likely to get sick or feel stress, if it is high, they are more capable of being happy and healthy.

REIKI is a simple, practical hands-on healing technique for deep relaxation. It can be learnt and practiced by anyone with a desire to improve health and well-being. It is the safest and simplest of natural alternative healing methods and yet it can bring profound, emotional, physical and spiritual relief. Reiki hands-on healing is one of the fastest growing therapies, not only in clinics but also in the home. Reiki allows us to become calmer and see the way forward with more clarity. The experience of healing allows people to regain lost vitality and to reassess their lives. Reiki allows us to become calmer and see the way forward with more clarity.

One of the greatest Reiki healing health benefits is stress reduction and relaxation which triggers the body's natural healing abilities and improves and maintains health. Reiki healing is a natural therapy that gently balances life energies and brings health and wellbeing to the recipient.

This simple, non-invasive healing system works with the Higher Self of the Receiver to promote health and wellbeing of the entire physical, emotional and psychic body. Therefore, it is truly a system of attaining and promoting wholeness of Mind, Body and Spirit. Reiki healing can be used safely with orthodox medicine and combines effectively with other complementary therapies such as massage, reflexology, counselling and many more.

Illness can be a time of great stress. Reiki can help us cope by encouraging relaxation and bringing balance to both mind and emotions. Reiki has been known to speed up recovery from surgery or long-term illness. It helps in adjusting to treatment; it also tends to reduce side-effects. For example, Chemotherapy patients who received Reiki noticed a marked decrease in side effects from treatment.

Meditation

There are many types of meditation. The one definition that fits almost all types of meditation reads: 'Consciously directing your attention to alter your state of consciousness.' The word meditation is derived from two Latin words: meditari 'to think', 'to dwell upon', and 'to exercise the mind' and mederi 'to heal'. Its Sanskrit derivation medha means 'wisdom'. With regular practice of a balanced series of techniques the energy of the body and mind can be liberated and the quality of consciousness can be expanded. This is not a subjective claim but is now being investigated by the scientists with exciting results.

When I want to meditate I put aside up to thirty minutes where I can sit and relax without being disturbed. Usually in a comfortable chair, or when I'm lying in bed before going to sleep. I find a spot on the wall or ceiling and focus my eyes on that point without blinking and hold my gaze, fixed, for as long as I can until I can't hold the gaze any longer. This is also a form of self-hypnosis. Once I have gently closed my eyes I focus on my breathing, slowing my breathing down until I find a balance, where breathing has become very easy and it takes no effort or awareness to breathe correctly. Breathing in through my nose and exhaling through my mouth.

Meditation practice in my experience is a technique to still our fleeting mind. Getting to know oneself and letting go of any of the day's events no longer required in your thoughts. One way I find very relaxing is to imagine that you're standing outside your body looking at yourself in detail. Starting at the top of your head and looking at it from an outside perspective, seeing if your scalp may be tense or taught. If it feels tense simply see it loosening and letting go of any tension or negativity. Slowly move down your body inspecting every area in detail, down from the forehead, eyes, lower neck, shoulders and arms, down your body; down to the tips of your toes. Take your time, please do not rush this.

Once you have achieved this, imagine the air in the room is full of millions of atoms of your favourite colour. See this colour clearly in your mind's eye and start to breathe it into your lungs. Breathing in through your nose and exhaling any negativity out of your mouth. Really see it and feel it as it enters your lungs and visualise it being distributed into your blood stream being directed around your body as if it was your own personal healing colour. Everywhere it touches, healing and relaxing, especially into all the muscle groups throughout your body.

Once you're feeling relaxed ask your subconscious for assistance. If you are in bed simply ask your subconscious what you want it to do whilst you are asleep. Simple suggestions like, while I sleep I will allow my body to let go of anything negative that may have happened today. Remind yourself that you cannot fail at being yourself or "I can never go back to yesterday because I was a different person then and tomorrow is a new day with a new start". This is one of my personal favourites. "I can and I will" and then put in what is the right context for yourself, e.g.; I can and I will feel energised when I awaken in the morning. I can and I will get my work completed tomorrow and I will feel good about it.

Try it, practice it and see what you can achieve using your inner thoughts, it's very powerful.

Growth from Birth

Is there anything nicer than a baby? The miracle of birth is in itself exactly what it says, a MIRACLE. For one cell to divide and grow into the person you are, goes way beyond science. To have the ability to see, touch, smell, sense, hear, and feel emotions. This goes, way, way above anything else and what do we do? We destroy it through our early teachings about beliefs.

We are brought into this world with a clear mind but from birth we are conditioned. This is a type of brain washing throughout our young developing growth, through religion or schooling and many others areas of control. We are not taught, or very few of us are taught about spirituality in the Western hemisphere. It is only a few years ago that my Aunt told me that my grandma and a number of my past family members were mediums. I had no idea because at that time, in my early childhood, it wasn't talked about, (people who 'dabbled' were 'a bit odd') and further back in time would have been branded a witch.

We are taught to remember and sometimes regularly reminded about things that have upset us. Maybe an embarrassing moment or silly incident we have experienced which makes us feel really bad, guilty, or hurt inside. It's no wonder some of us grow up with lots of repressions, in the subconscious and how they can externalise as fears, phobias, anxiety, etc. The mind is bombarded with suggestions, with rules and regulations from birth.

We need to be taught from an early age and at school about imagery and visualisation, and about balance and energy. Taught about chakras and what they mean, taught how to control thoughts and how to remain positive and not to allow negative feelings affect us. It has been taught in eastern countries for hundreds of years and at long last we are beginning to believe and take a bit more interest; it's about time.

I wasn't allowed to go into schools and teach young children because of the word Hypnosis but was given permission to take my aura camera to demonstrate to a couple of classes of fourteen year olds. After only an hour they understood a great deal more about chakras and energy and really enjoyed it; they even began analysing each other. The teacher told me later that she had never known them sit so still and take such an interest in anything before; even she enjoyed it.

Later in the book I will tell you about a new therapy I am now working with and how it can be used in schools successfully with both children and adults, without using hypnosis.

The following is a classic example of how things can be misunderstood by the mind because of certain belief systems. What is the opposite of love? I bet the majority of you replied, hate. Hate is not the opposite of love. It can't be because hate and love are both strong emotions. You cannot hate someone unless you care and if you're going to bring out the 'big guns' and stand throwing a tantrum, stamping your feet, screaming, "I don't love you anymore", I will tell you, right now, you are wrong.

The opposite of love is not hate but indifference. If you don't love someone anymore, it is because you have become indifferent to that person. We bring out the 'big guns', many times in our lives because we are hurt, upset and won't or don't want to face the inner truth. You have to listen and learn from that inner voice and reprogramme any negative thoughts through suggestion and visualisation.

I think it was the Americans who gave us the expression 'No pain, no gain' and I bet you also believe it is true. Well, it isn't, how can it be true? There is never any pain in growth, what is painful, is not growing. We can have misconceptions programmed into our subconscious minds from birth. Through life whilst you are 'growing in knowledge' there isn't any pain. The minute you stop growing then it becomes painful and the only way to get rid of the pain is to start growing again.

Everything you feel and experience comes from the inner voice. The one that never stops talking to you, it is important that you learn to listen. You do not think in words all the time, you think in images and it's the images you see of yourself that makes you become who you are. If your thinking is positive, then you will become positive; fact. The saying, 'you are what you think', is so true. I'm going to teach you how to listen closely to that inner voice and work on the image of yourself, through imagery and the inner voice.

Let me give you an example. About twenty years ago, I employed a new sales manager. He had been involved in sales for many years and was extremely good at his job. I couldn't understand why with such knowledge his monthly figures, did not increase. We had a meeting, I told him that when he joined my company he achieved a brilliant sales figure of four thousand pounds of new business and he had created a good new customer base.

The second month he could only work two weeks because of a prearranged holiday but he still achieved the sales of four thousand pounds. The third month, in four weeks, he achieved exactly the same figure again, four thousand pounds, so I asked him why? He replied, 'that's all I need'. His own imagery, his own inner voice had programmed him; that was all he could or wanted to achieve. It was obvious to me that it was his own self belief system which was holding him back and suggested that he tried a specific exercise for a week or longer. I asked him to go into the bathroom each morning and look into the mirror and say to himself with passion and energy: 'I like myself, I like myself, I'm the best salesman, I'm the best closer in this business, and I'm the best husband, the best lover'. I told him not to come out until he had repeated it for five minutes or longer. He even took it a step further and would repeat the affirmations whilst driving to work: 'I like myself, I like myself, and I am the best closer, best salesman', and so on.

After about seven days his attitude changed, he became much more positive and began to take on more responsibility. His personal presentation and sales skills improved and he soon passed the five thousand pound barrier.

It was all about his perception of himself, what he needed and what he was happy to settle for. He did make me laugh one day. He told me he had been sitting at traffic lights in Lancaster; he was in the left hand lane on the one-way system, waiting for the lights to change. He thought he'd practice his affirmations whilst waiting for the lights to change. Well, he was in full voice, very much involved in his imagery exercise, passionately chanting to himself, or so he thought. I like myself I'm best salesman, the best closer, the best husband. As he glanced to his right he could see a police car with two officers looking at him, very strangely. He had forgotten his window was down fully. So be careful where and when you do it. But it really does work. At least the Police didn't pull him over. Take a good look at yourself, what is it you would like to change about yourself, be honest? Never try to be someone or something you could never be.

Do you need to lose weight or stop smoking? Do you need more energy in your life? Is there something else you would like to change in areas of your life? Whatever area requires change it can only come from within you and your thoughts (the inner voice). Learn to listen to everything that comes from your inner voice, remember that child within. If it's negative, simply change it to something positive, keep doing this and you will change into the person you would like to become.

You own your mind and body, so take control of your thoughts. The mind commands the body obeys. Teach yourself to visualise the chakras in perfect balance but don't expect things to happen immediately. Keep practicing and repeating the imagery in the subconscious until it simply becomes a habit. Something you do without thinking. It is only difficult if you allow it to become difficult. So try it now.

If there has been sadness in your life and you're finding it difficult to cope, ask yourself, "Why" listen to the inner child and inner voice? What do you need to do to alter the energy and thoughts to make it better? You have a choice to remain in that energy and allow the chakras to become blocked and unbalanced or use effective imagery to balance the mind and body. I can look back through my life and think of the areas that caused me lots of anger, hurt and pain. Dwelling on those thoughts would have kept me in the past with that internal energy hurting inside. Learn to let go of it and reprogramme your mind by the inner thoughts and inner voice. If it means you have to forgive others for what has upset you in the past, just do it. Let go of it completely and stop taking things personally. It's your own imagery causing you pain and hurt.

Use the mirror technique, after a while people will notice a big change in you but be careful not to become too egotistical. Balance the new you and be aware of your new life.

Sometimes it can be as simple as learning to notice new things in everyday life, notice the things around you. Simply smiling at others we see and meet. Learning how to handle aggression, or jealousy, the list is endless. Don't be drawn into negativity through your own thoughts and inner speech because of someone else's negativity. It is a fact that you can make this life amazing, if you really want it to be, or maybe you would prefer to just wallow in self-pity. The old program is still chipping away; deep in your subconscious. Remove it, delete it and get rid of it. Now is the time to reprogramme. The human mind is an amazing tool, learn to use it, communicate with it, and communicate with your inner self.

Tell yourself that each day in every way you are going to feel better; better than you did yesterday but not as much as you are going to feel tomorrow. Learn to understand that your life is important and that you are going to listen and work with your inner voice. There are millions of things going on in your body and mind right now and you don't have to tell it what to do or how to do it. Be positive about the change that is going to happen and remember and become aware of the changes. Once you get onto that wheel of life you will be like the hamster that cannot get off. Make the effort to learn about yourself, get stuck into it, not just because you have to but because you want to.

The more you know, the more you will need and want to know. There are hundreds of books relating to these areas, all well worth reading.

Don't think you can do it without help, the majority of professionals and experts build up their knowledge from those who have gone before them.

Doctors cannot always be sure what is exactly wrong with a patient so they turn to one of their many reference books. Their shelves may hold over a hundred books, invested in over the years; their reference library. Okay, let me ask you, "How many books have you invested in, your own personal reference library? Not very many, is it?" Why do we feel we have to face things on our own? Millions of people have walked the road before us and have faced the same or similar problems we face every day. They have written solutions to those problems, written books for reference. If you try to do it alone it may take forever. There are many books with scripts teaching imagery and visualisation, teachings for relaxation. Relaxation and teaching CD's are readily available all over the internet, just google it. There are many thousands of books written relating to this area, as well as Metaphysical and Spiritual areas. Try to take that little bit of extra time to read and learn more about you.

If you wanted to lose weight or keep fit you'd join a gym, you would have an image in your mind of how you would like to look in the future.

If ever there was a time to change, when would that time be? I hope you replied "right now"; don't procrastinate, **DO IT**. Take a deep breath; see yourself, how you would like to be in three months' time. Make the imagery real and your mind will work towards it.

12. Life's Plan, Themes & Pathways

Before I go onto explain my views in this area I will make it clear, once again, they are only my views and you have the right to agree or disagree with any part of them.

The more people that I have worked with over the years, the more it has taught me that there is a link connecting the past life to this life. There is a theme to follow and a lesson to learn. It could be that in a past life, your life was cut short and the lesson was not finished or completed. Now you are back to experience another life to learn more and complete the lesson.

We come back as a new life but bring with us the lesson to be learned from our past.

Maybe, in a past life you were a husband or father. In this life you are female, married with children what could the lesson be? Perhaps, in your previous life you were a manipulative, domineering, overbearing controlling individual. In your new life you become the victim, experiencing how it feels to be manipulated, domineered, controlled and how it affects others' life 'lessons'! Over the years I have heard many people say, "I must have been horrible in my past to be experiencing the things that are happening to me right now." What do you think? Maybe, there could be something to it, after all, (but these are my thoughts and feelings based on years of my own and others experiences).

I have often wondered what my life's plan and theme is, so I asked for guidance from my guide Josh. I now fully understand what I have to learn and understand in this life. The word he gave me was PATIENCE. For years, in fact, as far back as I can remember, I have always been charged with energy. I was very impulsive. If I wanted something or to do something it had to happen immediately; I didn't want to wait. I was always in a rush. I wanted to 'run before I could walk'. After listening to Josh I have balanced myself out. I speak much more slowly and when I am working, I take my time and work at a more realistic speed. I am in control of my energy and what is my job now? Teaching people about balance and energy and helping them remove anxiety, stress, etc.

It was only after purchasing my aura camera and seeing for myself, my body's energy on the screen, that I realised I was close to burning out. I was getting older and feeling more like a 'drained battery'. I firmly believe that everyone has a pathway and theme to follow and working with auras and energy is just a small part of my theme. I also feel that in my other lives I have been a healer of some description and have returned to this life to use healing energy once again but also to learn and understand more about patience and to teach others.

What do you feel is your theme on Earth? What do you feel you have to learn and understand? Write your thoughts down and look at how and what you need to change to achieve this. Try relaxing and when you feel deeply relaxed just ask for your theme. You may be surprised what comes through. Look back through your life and see and feel how it connects to this present time.

I am not going to dwell on themes, pathways and lesson plans but try it out for yourself and experience where it takes you. I have done this with many people, under hypnosis and the replies have been extremely interesting.

Just recently a friend came for an aura reading and his reply after reading the report was. "I'm in a mess." At least he was wise enough to face the truth and he certainly needs to change a lot of things in his life to attain a better body balance and possibly live longer. It answered a lot of questions for him and hopefully he will learn and adjust to retain a much healthier life. It is never too late to change; your mind and body are more than capable to repair anything that needs to be repaired. It doesn't have to be difficult or hard, all you have to do is change a few thoughts and use imagery of how you would like to be and keep those thoughts clearly fixed in your mind. Your mind will work towards these and make it a reality. The mind commands the body obeys, it's a simple fact but so many of us are brought up in this life believing the opposite. Again, the old programme from the past is still working on you, subconsciously.

Have you ever had a very important meeting or interview to attend and had to be up very early in the morning to get ready and prepare yourself. You set the alarm clock the previous evening and arrange an early morning alarm call via the telephone just in case the alarm failed. I've had this experience many times in my life and guess what time I would wake, one minute before the alarm was set to go off. I think most of us have experienced something like this and it shows that you programmed the subconscious well and it carried out the programme you placed in your subconscious; there is no reason why you cannot do it for life itself. It must to be something that you know would benefit you and not something that you would never be able to achieve. Be realistic about your imagery and try not to do anything that you know will not work. Again, the more you repeat it in your thoughts the more your subconscious will create the imagery and make it a reality. If you only do it for a few days then it hasn't much chance of working so put stickers on the bathroom mirror or on the fridge to remind yourself to keep the thoughts and imagery focused. After approximately three weeks the subconscious should be working automatically; this means you will not have to think about it anymore. It will happen without you having to think about it and it will become simply a habit and a permanent programme. Don't forget that as a child this is how you learned things in school and in the work place; and those habits are still working away subconsciously right now. In schools, things are repeated all the time. Things have to be written down and gone over many times until they are learned and the memory remains in the subconscious for the rest of your life. Do you remember practicing and learning you're times tables at school? Some schools did them to music and you repeated and repeated until they became a habit.

Exactly the same thing will happen now as you reprogramme your subconscious for change and don't forget you were once an expert at doing it.

Mediumship and Clairvoyance

When people think of Mediums they often visualise people wearing long flowing robes, in a séance, sat round a table, with flickering candles holding hands with other people. They may visualise a darkened room and a crystal ball on a table. Many years ago mediums were killed for their beliefs as it was seen as a form of witchcraft and people were very scared of it.

Mediums are just ordinary people, usually with everyday jobs and families. A Medium is just a link between this world and the spirit world. Everyone has the capability of becoming a Medium, all that is required is a good teacher.

There are a number of forms of Mediumship:

Mediumship can be divided into two types, mental Mediumship and physical Mediumship. Mental Mediumship can be split into three more categories, Clairvoyance, Clairaudience and Clairsentience.

Mental Mediumship uses our psychic senses for the communication between the two worlds, whereas physical Mediumship endeavours to have those in the spirit world communicate through some physical means.

Clairvoyance

A person who is clairvoyant can see spirits. This usually means they see the person communicating in their mind's eye; this can be in the form of a picture or like watching a television in your head. Some mediums can see spirits with their physical eyes as if there is another person in the same room as themselves. The medium will then describe what they see to the person having the reading. It is not always people that mediums see; it can also be animals or even objects and symbols related to the person having the reading. Some objects will be given to the medium to be interpreted symbolically. I sometimes get animals coming in strongly when I'm reading.

Clairaudience

With this form of Mediumship the person hears the spirit communicating with them. Again, this can be voices in the Medium's head or thoughts running through the mind. Sometimes a Medium will actually hear someone talking to them with their physical ears. The Medium will not only "hear" voices, but can also be given music or singing. I personally don't get sounds but I get senses of sounds or songs.

Clairsentience

This in some schools of Mediumship is the most common form and experienced very often by people just beginning to understand the gift they have. This type of Mediumship takes the form of the Medium sensing a spirit presence, usually through feelings. Mediums often feel as if they are being touched, feelings of cold or slight breezes wafting past them. Sometimes they can have the feeling of cool air on the face or can even smell and sense fragrances associated with the spirits presence of their time on earth. I often get the perfume of Lily of the Valley so I know it's my mother linking with me or letting me know she is around. I always feel coldness in my legs as Josh connects with me and helps me to channel.

Mediums will use one or more of these forms of communication in order to convey messages from the spirit world and when a Medium is channeling and linking to the spirit, it is very important to give exactly what is being seen or felt. Sometimes you get images in your mind or thoughts that don't seem to make any sense or have any relevance whatsoever. But you will be surprised at times, how much of what you had been seeing has a meaning, or a link to the person you are reading and channeling for. I have not been doing this sort of channeling very long but I know that I will get better with more practice.

One day as I was taking a break from writing I decided to go and try a little bit of fishing down by the port, (Spain). I find fishing relaxes me and it gave me time away from the computer where I could sit and think about the direction of my book. I was sat with my legs dangling over the stone jetty, just watching my float bobbing up and down in the sea when a woman walked towards me and said, "I like fishing" and that was the start of a very interesting conversation. She looked me and said, "I'm so sorry I have no idea why I came up to you and told you that because normally I am very shy and say nothing." She asked what I did in my work and it wasn't long before we were discussing various areas of spirituality. I started linking to her neck, so I asked her if she had any problem in that area. I asked her permission and placed my finger where she was having problems; I was being drawn to her left shoulder, close to the base of the neck. She asked how I knew as it was exactly where she had been suffering pain for years.

She excitedly shouted her husband to join us. She was amazed that I had pin pointed the exact area. After explaining about my energy work I asked if I could place my hands over the area and see what I could pick up. When I finished my healing I asked her to move her neck and tell me how it felt. She was quite emotional, the pain and all the tension had gone completely from her neck and shoulder. She went into more detail about how her husband had to rub in a painkilling cream every night before she could sleep. I was linking to her extremely well and asked her permission to continue. All I could see in my mind were babies. I passed on this information and she laughed saying, "Well I am a midwife and have delivered hundreds of babies." I then linked to a Daffodil and linked to a name, it was her Grandma standing over my shoulder and a very young male child stood with her. It turned out that she had lost a little boy early in a pregnancy and here he was in my mind, stood with Grandma. I gave her everything I could hear, feel and sense; every word and it was perfectly accurate. It gave her closure on what she had carried inside for years. It's at times like that I totally love everything about my work. That woman will change and blossom more as her life progresses, without any pain returning to her neck area. Meeting her happened for a reason and it is something I totally believe in. Out of all the thousands of people on holiday and the many, many people who visit the port area, she was drawn directly to me. Spirit certainly guided us together that day.

I was told several years ago that I would become and work as a Medium. I certainly couldn't see that happening but now I am linking and starting to move towards mediumship and clairvoyance work as well as my aura camera work and past lives.

Over the years I have heard arguments about people charging for readings. In my work, I do charge for hypnotherapy, past life regressions, and aura readings. Should my direction include clairvoyance or mediumship I will have to charge something. I do have to live and have bills and expenses like everyone else but the one thing I never charge for is healing, or laying of hands. Spirit gave me this direction and it is my way of giving something back to spirit and that is how it will always remain. I certainly would never enter into arguments regarding what others charge. It's so sad to see many people in the same profession arguing with each other over money and charges. Some of the charges are astronomical. I only wish I could give my spiritual work for free but that is not possible all the time, nor is it feasible, so I try to keep my charges as fair as possible; this is of course, my choice.

I was going to spend time talking about Tarot cards but the truth is that I know so little about them that I would have to use information written by others. It is about my journey of spirituality. I have really never been involved in the area of Tarot reading except for one thing that happened to me a few years ago regarding cards. A friend gave me a pack of cards she had personally made for me and asked me to give her a reading using them. The cards as I said were individually made and had pictures on both sides. She selected three cards and asked me to look at the picture on one side only and to look deeply into the picture and give what I could see and feel. This I did, three cards, six pictures and it just seemed to flow. I gave what I could see in the pictures and how it was connected to her. I apparently gave a very accurate reading and was totally stunned by it. I haven't done much with the cards since and they are still here inside the bag specially made for them by a dear friend. It is decorated with a butterfly and made of blue silky material. On one side it has the initials T.W.W. embroidered into it. These are the initials of my screen name, Tewka White Wolf. I have used this name for over fifteen years and many, many people know me online by this name. I will possibly be using the cards in the near future and they will become another tool in my spiritual progress.

Years ago my wife and I owned and ran a hotel on the north-west coast of Scotland and this is where I was introduced to computers and the internet. I knew very little about computers, I didn't even know how to switch them on never mind use one. It was funny trying to find the letters on the keyboard just to type my name. It wasn't one of the easiest things for me, especially as I am dyslexic. After a few weeks of being taught how to connect to a chat program I was communicating with people from all over the world via the AOL server. This was in the days of 'dial up connection' and the immortal words when you eventually connected to the internet, (Welcome to AOL.) At that time, connections weren't brilliant and I seemed to spend a lot of time rebooting my computer and trying to reconnect after crashing time and time again.

The first chat programme I used was called ICQ and the first person I spoke to, or should I say typed to was a lady in Canada. It was just utterly amazing seeing the text replies on my screen, appearing in seconds. Answers to questions I typed to someone thousands of miles away. It wasn't long before we became quite good friends and often spent a few hours chatting via the ICQ program; learning more about each other and our families. I chatted via type to many people from all over the world and used to enjoy the different views and opinions of people from all walks of life. They would type back about their interest in past lives and my work in Hypnotherapy and analysis.

As the internet progressed many chat rooms were formed, microphones could now be used, the ability to speak to people in the rooms and share views. Many of the larger servers had created their own chat rooms and anyone could enter. It used to be fun sitting in spiritual rooms listening to all the different subjects being discussed regarding spirituality or metaphysical subjects. I suppose this is where my first connections to spiritually really began. There would be rooms about Angels, Mediums, Clairvoyants, Tarot Cards, Crystals, Light workers, Energy workers, Chakra readers, Remote Viewing, Crystal balls, Guides, Past Lives, virtually every area of spiritualism or metaphysical subjects were discussed. I used to sit and listen for hours to many gifted readers and teachers on chat programmes.

A friend introduced me to another type of chat room that had become available and it wasn't long before I had it loaded onto my computer and sat in the spiritual rooms once again listening to the many and varied discussions. This program suited me much better; technology had really progressed. Connections were much stronger with the introduction of ASDL and this particular programme had very good voice clarity. I opened my own chat room in time using the title "Tewka's Past Life Regression Room" and many evenings the room would be very busy with thirty or more people in it. They were listening to me discussing my work on past lives and hypnotherapy. I used to have many teachers coming into the room talking about their journey with spirit. The rooms used to have Admins who helped to control and monitor the text within the room. The Admins were selected by the room owner and should anyone come in and try to destroy the energy or be rude and disrespectful to any of the readers the administrators would 'red dot' them. This simply meant that the intruder couldn't type or speak in the room again and usually they were asked to leave. If they refused they were bounced out of the room instead. We now had a programme we could control and one that allowed us to monitor the type of person we allowed into the room.

Some evenings I would lock the room to outsiders and only invite my friends. I would teach about past lives or explain my views on imagery and visualisation. It was also possible to play music for others to listen to and it gave me the idea of playing some of my relaxation classes CD's; I also gave live relaxation techniques. Most of the time I would teach imagery and often end up with ten people in a locked room (the maximum allowed), relaxing them into a hypnotic session. At the end of every session people would share their views on how much more relaxed they now felt compared to before and the tension and stress they had prior to the session was now gone. The internet had now opened up such a wide area for me regarding my therapy work; it was now possible to help and teach many people from all over the world.

I used to have many teachers come into my room and run classes on mediumship or classes on how to work with energy or how to connect to a guide or guides. We also had regular discussions about Angels and their role in our daily lives.

It was a time in my life which taught me so much about spirituality and it was on the same chat room programme that I first met Walks with Spirits, (Rick)

Over the years I spent a lot of time in a private room listening to his views on spirituality and he without a doubt became the biggest influence in my spiritual work. He was a fantastic teacher with a massive knowledge of spirituality in many areas. He was also very direct about his views and simply 'didn't take any prisoners', you either listened to him or he would not waste his time or energy. Over the years on this chat programme Walks made many friends and influenced so many for the better. Many people remember him because of his wicked sense of humour, he was an expert at teasing and winding people up. When he was online, you would see different "away messages" after his screen name saying things like "get off my internet" even typing this about him is making me smile. He is sadly missed by so many. Walks could also be a bit of a flirt but it was all harmless fun. Some evenings when I was chatting to him in private he would also speak to my wife doing a little tiger growl at her and really teasing her.

Over the years, a very fond and strong friendship developed between Jaqui and Rick and we talked about going over the Pond (Atlantic) to visit him one day. Sadly, he passed away before we could realise that wish. When he died it was such a sad loss for everyone but he has certainly left his mark.

On one of my early websites was a Walks with Spirit memorial page, R.I.P. my dear friend.

Unfortunately, over the years, this chat program and the energy changed. Many of the rooms either fell out amongst themselves, using nasty, hurtful words or making direct attacks on peoples' views. It saddens me, a few of the people I used to know being so disrespectful to spirit. They have in my mind, lowered themselves in spiritual energy rather than growing and developing more. It has now become so egotistical in some of the rooms and more like a battleground rather than a place to learn. I used to sit and listen to superb teachings. I feel it's about time some of these people grew up and stopped tearing down others. Perhaps they will then stop doing it to themselves. Karma will play its part here no doubt but it is such a shame it had to happen in the first place.

I have recently reopened my room on past lives and many people have had the same thoughts as me. Where have all the good rooms gone, what is happening to all the energy now? The room I opened was full of lovely people, with twenty or more coming in and having an interesting room discussing various metaphysical and spiritual topics; just like we used to. It wasn't long though before the idiots came in under different nicknames, to hide their true identity and once again being silly and stupid and disrupting the energy.

Nowadays, I have a few special friends who I occasionally chat to in a private room and keep up with what's been happening in their lives. Without the internet, this simply wouldn't have happened and the chat rooms available are sometimes such a lifeline for so many people who are housebound or simply cannot get out.

Without the chat rooms I certainly would not have had the direction or knowledge I have now in my spiritual work, so things certainly do happen for a reason.

Many times I have had the opportunity to go into a private room and because of the internet, not only can I speak to that person, I can now see them on my screen, via a webcam (of course with their permission). This enables me to get a link to the energy of that person and for me to do my healing work. The internet has become a link for many spiritual people to assist in various areas; helping people they would normally have never been able to meet or see before.

It is strongly recommended, especially regarding illnesses, that you always consult a doctor before doing anything.

There are many sites of professional readers on the internet offering readings but ask for money before commencing the reading. I have absolutely no problem with any of them but I would suggest that you look for letters and recommendations, or comments left by others on their websites before making any kind of decision. Unfortunately there are still a number of Charlatans out there. I have even witnessed it, in one chat room; a lady was taking individuals from her main chat room into a private room and carrying out a free reading. She had many people waiting for their reading but what she was doing in the private room was telling people that they were governed and covered by a dark entity of energy. The person was then told that this energy needed to be cleansed or they may die but of course she would have to charge for this service because of the energy involved in removing it. The amount she was asking was over one hundred dollars and some people actually paid her because they were so scared and believed in what she had said. It wasn't long before a number of people on the chat programme realised what was happening and notified the owners. They duly removed her from the programme completely and the police were contacted. So please be careful, there are charlatans out there willing to take your hard earned money.

13. The Return Home

As you have read earlier in this book I have lived in Spain twice. The second time I was hoping to set up some work with my hypnotherapy and aura camera. This would have a financial income so my wife could retire from her school work in the UK and join me in Spain. We decided not to sell our property, just in case things didn't work out in Spain. We could always return back to the UK, should we ever need to.

For about a year things went well, then the recession hit Spain. It was just as if someone had hit a light switch and turned it off.

The construction industry stopped and buildings were just being left unfinished. The locals were finding things extremely difficult and could not find work. After a long lengthy discussion with Jaqui, it was decided that I should return to the UK. I returned in June, just prior to Jacqui's birthday; we were both totally fed up and extremely disappointed. We have been back since for holidays and the economy still hasn't picked up. Friends we made over there are still struggling to make ends meet.

It was during the latter part of being in Spain that I noticed I was getting lots of pain deep down in my lower back which went into both legs as I walked. It seemed to be getting worse and was affecting my walking; in a way it was good that I had returned back to the UK. I often wonder if it was Spirit that brought me back, or was it just a fact I had to accept. Getting heath care in Spain would have been very expensive and with little money would have been virtually impossible.

The pain in my back increased considerable and I had several MRI's and X-rays. I was also given several injections in my lower back but nothing seemed to help. The consultant found that where the veins branched off from the main veins into my legs were virtually blocked. Very little blood was getting through into my legs which meant there was only a faint pulse in my lower leg. The pain this caused was becoming difficult to bear. I was prescribed neuro blockers and very strong pain killers including morphine but again, nothing helped. The surgeon then decided he would perform a procedure whereby stents would be inserted into the arteries via both groins. This was supposed to increase the blood flow to my legs but the procedure didn't seem to alter things very much. After yet more MRI's and tests, it was decided I would need major surgery to correct the problem; a bi-femoral bypass. It was to be a six to eight hour operation and artificial veins would be used to bypass the blockages in both arteries. It had taken four years; very difficult four years. I had reached the stage where the pain in my back was becoming unbearable and I was unable to walk more than a few yards without having to stop and wait for the pain to leave my legs before I could carry on. This is one of the reasons I decided to go back to my hypnotherapy work once more. I could work from home, as and when I felt well enough.

During this time, and I have left this part deliberately for the ending of my book, something happened that was to change my life completely. It just blew me away.

This is going to be exciting because I have so much to say about it and hopefully you will try it, see it, and feel it for yourself. It's awesome, it really is.

As I mentioned previously, I have been a qualified therapist for over 30 years and have been trained on many areas of application, Direct Suggestion, NLP, Analytical therapy, Bio-Feedback and many more modalities.

I was introduced to this new approach to a therapy called PSTEC and click tracks, the results of which have been outstanding. This time it is based on science but somehow I feel it's helped me so much more with my spirituality and in the helping of others.

PSTEC (Percussive Suggestion Technique)

Nearly four years ago a friend of mine sent me a web link, something he thought I would find interesting. It was a different and new type of therapy approach. I glanced at it, saved it to my favourites and completely forgot about it for about least three weeks.

When I eventually opened it I thought, at first, it was a type of EFT, Emotional Freedom Technique. It couldn't have been further from the truth, as I was to find out. The site was offering a completely free download. I downloaded it straight away and listened to the easy to follow instructions.

After listening to the owner's audio introduction I became very intrigued and willing to give this new technique a try. After all I had nothing to lose, it was FREE and you cannot get anything better than free.

The Click Tracks

On the click tracks you are asked to find something to work on. Something connected to an emotion, such as, anxiety, a fear, or maybe a phobia, self-confidence, insecurity, stress, in fact anything connected with an emotion. You are then asked to give it a number on a scale of naught to ten; ten being the highest it could possibly be. Once you have done that you listen to the click track and follow everything that you are asked to do. It couldn't be any easier.

I eventually found something; I had a fear of being on a ladder. As I got closer to the top my legs would turn to jelly which in turn made me feel extremely anxious; but I didn't have a fear of heights. Simple things like painting or cleaning out the gutters became a nightmare as I simply couldn't do it without experiencing that awful feeling. I got the old memory into my thoughts and followed the click track. I started off on number nine and after one playing; the number had gone down to zero.

I sat there a little bit bewildered after the session. I couldn't understand what had happened and as much as I tried to get that memory/emotion back, I simply couldn't. It was a lovely relaxed feeling and the strange thing is I knew it had left me. I felt totally different. If I thought of being up a ladder there was no longer any negative emotion there.

After that initial session I think it was about two weeks later that my wife informed me that the birds had blocked the guttering on the side of the house. I duly went, got the ladders, climbed right to the top and cleaned out the guttering and then of course descended. I was carrying the ladders to put them back into my garage when it suddenly dawned on me what I had just done. If there was ever proof needed and to know if the click tracks had worked, it was then. Just to make sure I took the ladders back and went up them again without any fear or anxiety.

That was my eureka moment and since then and for the last four years I have been using nothing else in my therapy work. It's been one amazing journey and to have such tools now to help others is possibly one of the greatest gifts I have ever received. I am also very proud to call myself a PSTEC Master Practitioner.

Why haven't I heard of this before?

This is a cutting edge psychological tool which was only released four years ago. It has been used by thousands of people around the world and the results have astonished both therapists and clients. Its creation was drawn from a number of fields including artificial intelligence, linguistics, hypnosis, and conditioned responses. Knowledge of these unrelated fields paved the way for a unique "model" of the mind to be developed. This allowed for the identification of how the subconscious generates emotion and processes language. This in turn allowed for the creation of a quick mechanism with which to undo the conditioned fear response. Despite its relative "newness" the use of this technique is spreading like wild fire and we predict that in the very near future this will be a standard feature and tool used by self-helpers and therapists alike. Of course, state introduction of brand new therapies can be laboriously slow, so it may be a few years before governments and mental health departments have little choice but to sit up and take notice of this psychological revolution which is happening right under their noses.

Easily Relieve Stress, Limit Anxiety, Eliminate Phobias and much more

Discover a non-chemical means of soothing destructive memories, to relieve stress, limit anxiety, and eliminate phobias, amongst other benefits. If you don't try it, you will never experience the amazing predictable results PSTEC can **offer.**

Transformation within Minutes

This may sound like something straight out of your favourite science-fiction movie, such as Eternal Sunlight for the Spotless Mind, but it's quite real and requires no unheard-of technology or harmful drugs. Instead, this rapid and effective 'desensitisation' is facilitated by listening to intelligently designed audio tracks.

Rather than write more about this revolutionary therapy, it's better if you go to my website and download the free tracks and try them out for yourself. I will put some of the testimonials I have received regarding the use of the click tracks for you to read in a later chapter.

Get your Free click track downloads at :

www.mwhypno.co.uk._

My work with Children in Schools

I had been working with the click tracks for about six months with superb success. During a chat with my wife one evening we decided click tracks would be beneficial to students who were struggling with emotional issues in school. I must point out, that to work with children I had to obtain a special license from the owner and creator of PSTEC. I spoke to Tim and after lengthy discussions and because of my previous background and knowledge of hypnotherapy working with children this was authorized and a license duly given.

I gave a twenty minute talk to several members of staff, this included the headteacher, deputy heads and four other staff members. They had a short private discussion and I was invited to work with a few children on a three month trial basis two mornings a week.

For slightly over two years I worked at the school with numerous children and staff. The children were simply amazing and I built up a special relationship with those who came to see me and the results were truly astonishing. During that time I worked with many issues, including self-harm, exam nerves, stress and anxiety issues, fears, phobias, anger and guilt, two attempted suicides, bullying, and many more. As I saw more and more children the word spread. I even heard one student say, go and see Magic Mike, he will help you. How gratifying was that?

I found out that most schools had a range of therapists available to work with the children but were only teaching coping strategies. No one was working at a subconscious level and providing emotional clearance.

Over time I came to understand that children's issues were far greater than I had ever imagined. Life was fast and stressful for many of them and to be involved and helping them was just brilliant. Ridding them of all the garbage they had picked up during their short lives, never to affect them again in the future.

Unfortunately, my work in school came to an end. Alas, the head teacher and deputy head teacher were leaving the school to move on to pastures new.

The new head teacher didn't want to continue with my services; the reason given was lack of funding. I was very sad and disappointed as I had a great rapport with many of the children and staff, but there was nothing I could do. Strange, but there you go, some people are very reluctant to change. It's the children and teachers who suffer long term.

I am extremely proud that I was the first person to work in a school with children, teachers and families using the PSTEC therapy system in the UK; it has opened the door for others to follow. Because of my success a colleague and friend of mine, another PSTEC Master Practitioner, who lives approximately one hour south of me has begun working with a number of schools using the PSTEC system; again with fantastic results.

It's just a matter of time before it will be available for every school in the UK. To have children benefit from this would be the icing on the cake for me. PSTEC is amazing, fast and is permanent.

I have gained a good understanding of how schools work and what you must and must not do. I worked closely with the child protection officer at all times and before she left the school I received this lovely letter from Barbara, (Deputy Head Teacher) about my work in the school.

TESTIMONIALS

To Whom It May Concern,

Mike Wells – PSTEC

It has been Heysham High School's very great pleasure to have worked with Mike Wells now for almost two years.

Mike first come to our attention after much corporate head scratching about how best to address some of the very complex issues we were experiencing with a small number of students who had quite deeply rooted insecurities, fears and phobias about education. Often they would present as very angry young people who frequently refused to comply with any instructions, would walk out of the classrooms and truant and would be very verbally challenging. Contact with home usually revealed that parents were exhausted with their children's behaviour and unable to manage it. The universal services we had at our disposal were having no impact if we could engage them and it was becoming extremely difficult to successfully refer into the rapidly dwindling outside agencies. In addition, our capacity to fund services was becoming under threat.

Mike's work is very simple in many ways although the theoretical bases to it are founded on a sophisticated understanding of emotional development, neurology, psychology and physiology. Mike uses a "Click Track" method whereby his clients are guided through a series of personal reflections and though processes whilst responding simultaneously to tone based manual activity instructions: the "clicks". His techniques are unique. The use of ICT as a delivery medium immediately intrigues and engages the young person and there is no requirement of extended dialogue, something that these particular children find difficult and intimidating.

From a purely lay person's point of view and with apologies to the experts, PSTEC work by using subliminal repetitions to re-programme and re-set some of the brain's emotionally triggered pathways and synapses. It is unlike any therapy I have ever seen in operation previously. A significant number of our children, their parents and our staff have tried it and fed back some staggering results. The success rates are high.

I would recommend Mike without hesitation to you if you are looking for a no-nonsense approach unblocking some of the barriers that your young people may be experiencing to their engagement with education. Best of all, Mike is flexible about time scales, can work in school or peripatetically and does not require a mountain of paperwork to have been completed before he can engage with the young person. He is also happy to work on a total family basis. He is very discrete and highly professional. His charges and tariffs are also very attractive and flexible. Mike has been a valuable addition to our support team. Above all, he is a splendid chap with a pragmatic understanding of how schools work and the unpredictable nature of the beast.

B Manning

Deputy Head Teacher/Head of Inclusion

***

Already steps are being made to make PSTEC available to every school in the UK, via a license, all due to our early pioneering work.

Very soon we will be moving forward into the NHS to help people with high anxiety issues, panic attacks and of course many other high emotional issue areas. The list is endless how PSTEC could and would help.

***

Agoraphobia sufferer:

Thank you so much for introducing me to this wonderful, amazing yet simple technique called PSTEC and spending precious time in guiding me through two of my big issues. Throughout the Clicking Tracks, I seemed to let go of the first issue easier than the second. During the first issue which was connected to the recent events at work that have caused a lot of anxiety I realised that it melted almost three quarters of the way. At the end of the session I couldn't give monkeys about the whole saga. I am facing this saga on the 24th of September and will e-mail you how I felt through the upcoming anxiety ridden event. The second issue concerning eating disorder was a little harder to crack as I feel that it was somewhat deeper rooted? Nevertheless the feeling did fade to a much lower number on the scale and I felt much more at ease with the issue. I would strongly recommend PSTEC and the click tracks to all who are willing to open their minds and hearts and try this for themselves and actually take responsibility to heal and move on into a better way of existence. Looking forward eagerly to going through some more issues with you Mike, it feels like this could be perfect soul spring clean. Thank you again Mike and blessings, light and love to you for sharing this with the sleepy world.

Hi Mike I just wanted to say thank you for your help. I would not be aware of the amazing technique you shared with us last night; the person who has invented it is a miracle worker.

I did go out this morning at first with hubby as I was very unsure, I did however go to a shop alone which was a good distance from hubby something I have never attempted in over 35 years alone so I was thrilled to bits with myself, I stood in the line at the till and paid for my things and felt 10ft tall (ha, ha I am only 4ft-11ins).

I have looked at the site and hubby has been reading also, I am going to order the CD this week.

Just wanted to let you know I did go out as I told you I would, I am extremely grateful. Thanks a million bye for now ***Chris x***

***

I have suffered from extreme nerves regarding needles or injections, even the sight or talking about it then sent a cold shiver down my spine. This has progressively worsened over a ten year period. This meant anytime a dentist or doctor were needed or advised I found excuses or suddenly got better!

Today I had no choice but to visit my doctor for a lingering illness and after the consultation he said the dreaded words "Blood Test". In my desperation my partner organised an emergency session with Mike Wells of Morecambe Hypnotherapy Centre for a PSTEC session, prior to the test- 45 minutes later I felt strangely relaxed. The blood test seemed not to be important and did not make my guts lurch as normal. Less than 2 hours later I had given blood without any of the dizziness, sickness and generally chronic stress that usually came with it (despite waiting outside the Nurses door for 10 minutes too!) I am a logical person who likes to know facts before I believe anything, sceptic if you like, but I would recommend this treatment as strongly and highly as I could. Stop suffering and start living! **Andrew**

***

Where do I start? When I came to see you I had no idea how much of a mess I was really in. So many things in my life had gone so wrong and I felt worthless inside.

I thought the click tracks were silly to start with and certainly wouldn't work for me, but I got the biggest shock ever after the first session. After three sessions my life has changed so much for the better, all the guilt and anger I had been carrying from early childhood has GONE. And what's more I know it isn't going to upset me ever again.

I have recommended a few people to come and see you. If I only had known about this amazing new approach ten years ago I certainly wouldn't have had to go through all that pain that was in my life. Tim has designed something that will change people's lives forever for the better. I cannot thank you enough.

I came to see you today regarding my fear of flying. Before my session I would definitely say that my fear of flying on a scale of one to 10 would have been 100. The thought of getting on a plane would instill such fear that I would panic. If I thought about a plane or flying I would get clammy hands and the hairs on my neck would stand on end. Immediately after my session I felt calmer and I know it sounds completely unbelievable but when I think about flying or planes I just see it as another mode of transport, I don't become agitated – in fact I really couldn't care less about it and if I were to give my fear a number rating now would be a minus.

Many thanks. Georgie

***

Hi Mike

First I would like to say thank you for taking the time to help me! Before the click track I wasn't sleeping to well with everything that was on my mind, I felt low and not fully focused although not depressed! after we did the click track all of it was released which left me positive and focused in a way I needed to be, I'm now looking forward to my new journey with happiness and joy in all ways, which has also left me now to be excited! anyone who hasn't tried the click track I would say go for it don't let yourself feel confused or however you feel through situations in life break free from your attachments set yourself free!

***

Hi Mike this is Mag's daughter Debbie. Just to say thank you for the C/D. This helped me very much; I used the C/D about three times leading up to my operation and once on the morning of my operation. In the morning when I got to the hospital I was so chilled out and whilst waiting to go down I would click my hands on my lap to myself and think of the c/d, still feeling chilled out. I went through the operation with no problems. This C/D gave me a wonderful feeling of feeling spaced out and chilled, relaxed and not to worry about anything, for better words. "What will be, will be" I recommend this C/D to anybody to try it, go with an open mind because it really works. I will use it once a week just to chill me out as I have three children and a hectic life and always on the go. Once again, thank you, AMAZING. **Much Love Debbie**

***

I was stressed about exams and the feeling of failure, so I went to see Mike Wells - before my Biology exam - he spoke to me about my feelings and introduced me to the click tracks. I found it brilliant. Before the click tracks, on a scale of one to ten and ten being the worst, I felt eight, because of the stress and pressure to do well in school and get good grades was unbearable. During the click track I could sense a change that suddenly a weight had been lifted from my shoulders and instead of feeling pressure and stressed I felt relieved and happy. I went into my Biology exam with smiles across my face knowing that I had nothing really to worry about! It went well too, I was able to answer all of the questions provided and I will get my results in August and I am hoping to achieve a B or above. If I do, it will be because of the click track.

Before I knew I was able to have the click track before my exam, I knew I wasn't able to get through the exam. However, now I feel a lot happier and back to my normal self now.

Thank you Mike and the Click Tracks, Hannah

***

Before the session I had with Mike, I always felt anxious when faced with a certain situation and it was crippling my abilities in school and admittedly I had my doubts as to whether PSTEC would work. Any skepticism was completely gone about a quarter of the way through the session, when I noticed the effects of it; I was even smiling halfway through.

Afterwards, it felt like a weight had been lifted from my shoulders and what feelings I had ever had were gone. This will help me in many situations from now on and I will whole heartedly advocate this treatment to anyone stressed or extremely anxious, as I was.

***

Hi Mike

I've been using the free click track for my social anxiety, and "agoraphobia." I don't know whether or not I would be clinically diagnosed, but situations involving neighbours over the last few years have caused a lot of anxiety, and depression; to the point where I was almost terrified to leave my house. So bad to where I had to have my partner with me every time I go out. I had to use the back door even to take out the rubbish. Anyway, it is definitely improving with using the click tracks. I've been going to the shop on my own, quite comfortably. Got out and cleared up the garden. I can take my dogs out. It's really great. The thoughts that I used to have just don't seem to be there. Over all I would describe it as just feeling natural, and whole. Something I haven't felt for years. I think it's so awesome you're offering this all for free to people. Like I said I've passed on the URL to a few people I thought could use it. Hopefully they get as much out of it as I am.

Oliver

***

Mike: In March 2012 I was signed off work with depression, panic disorder which led to Agoraphobia and also Claustrophobia. This stress had a massive impact on my life as I couldn't go out not even to do shopping. In January of this year I was recommended to go and see Mike Wells a PSTEC Therapist. I wasn't sure at first if it would help me as I had suffered so long. After the first session I went out with my dogs, walking for over two hours and after my second session I felt great I was back driving and shopping. I am also now looking for a job. I would totally recommend Mike Wells and the use of PSTEC and because of him I now have my life back. I cannot thank him enough. ***Mike C***

***

I visited Mike and experienced the "click track system". I was suffering a debilitating fear of heights when skiing and this was spoiling my long awaited holidays and the highlight of my year. I really had tried to overcome this fear and at a point where I was considering not going again. At first I was not sure it had worked but as soon as I was on the slopes I was so calm and I experienced no fear at all. The fear had turned into "gosh that was hard but it was no problem." I can't recommend this system enough and will be singing its praises and using it again where I can.

***

A far as I can remember I have always been an anxious, stressed person and a constant worrier, I would always be able to see and feel the worse of a situation even before it had happened. Over the past year the anxiety has defiantly taken over my life, it has resulted in feelings of panic, low self-esteem, dread and physical symptoms such as muscular pain in neck and shoulders along with upset stomach quiet often. All of this was affecting my day to day life, work and especially my relationship with my partner that I decided to go to the doctors to discuss this. I was diagnosed with a generalised anxiety disorder and was offered a number of medications; I decided to decline the medication as I felt these would only mask my symptoms and not resolve the underlying problem.

***

In April 2013 I was pointed in the direction of Mike Wells through a close friend after hearing about the work he does with the PSTEC Click Tracks. I was very apprehensive at first and worried about how it all worked. I also felt that the click tracks would not work on me as this anxiety had been a part of my life for a long time and in the past year had only got worse resulting in more symptoms.

In my first session I discussed with Mike the problems I face and the things I feel and some of my past history, he was very sympathetic and reassured me that the PSTEC Click Tracks would help. I was asked on a scale of 1 – 10 (10 being the worst) on how the anxiety makes me feel, I decided it was about a 9. After doing the PSTEC Click Tracks Mike asked the same question again and how I felt was about a 2 and I was able to think about the things that made me anxious before but I wasn't able to bring up the strong physical feelings that came with it before!!!

I have had two sessions with Mike and can honestly now say that I feel a million times better than I have ever felt before, I am looking forward to enjoying what the future holds for me knowing that if something does occur in life that causes me worry or anxiety I now have the tools (click tracks) to use at home whenever I need.

Thank you Mike for your support, your understanding and the click tracks to use at home and most of all for changing my future for the better.

A Personal Message from Mike regarding PSTEC

I feel PSTEC is going to revolutionise therapy in the years to come, mainly because of its simplicity for the user and the amazing results it achieves. Thousands of people are now getting more involved with the PSTEC system. I also believe very strongly that Tim, the owner and creator of PSTEC has given a gift to the world. He continually improves and brings out more amazing programmes. I believe schools will use PSTEC in the future as will health services world-wide as more and more people become aware of this new revolutionary therapy. It has to happen and it will happen. It will help many people to become free from stress and anxiety and help them in other areas of their lives without the use of drugs or expensive invasive one to one therapy.

PSTEC is predictable because it is based on science.

Download the PSTEC Click Tracks and try it for yourself. The new 2015 Click Tracks are available via my website.

14. The Final Chapter

We have covered many different areas and topics I have been fortunate to be involved in during my thirty plus years of spiritual and metaphysical growth.

I could have gone into much more detail but for now I've tried to keep it simple and give you an insight into my work and experiences over the years.

There is no doubt the Earth is evolving more spiritually and Metaphysically each day. People are experiencing intense changes in their lives, work, behaviours and personal relationships. Many are awakening at a rate that can only be described as phenomenal. From spirituality, the aura camera, past lives, etc., right up until this present day using PSTEC; if I had to pick one area that has had the biggest impact on my life and others lives, then it would have to be PSTEC and the click tracks. Spirituality has nothing to do with religion as you already possibly know. It is knowledge, your divine inner-self and relearning to listen to that inner voice and that inner child and to let it guide you.

Nothing "spiritually" comes from without. Spirituality can only come from that which has always been within. Unfortunately, we are conditioned through beliefs to look outside to leaders, religious institutions, science, education, etc., to discover what we are supposed to be. It is tough to find the divine amidst all the noise of this conditioning. I simply could not be where I am today if it wasn't for the spirituality that guided me towards PSTEC and its science. It is a 'Mind Blowing' FACT.

We all can be healers in some form and we all have the ability within us. We all have that choice. It is what I call Free Will. So enjoy your pathway and while you're walking it, enjoy everything around you; do not take things for granted. Embrace this short life because as you get older you will realise that time has no meaning. This lifetime goes so fast; like a blink of one's eye. I know because I'm experiencing it every day. You may not be there yet but it will happen to you one day and you may just remember my words. Enjoy the rest of your life and become aware of your own reality and remember: Don't just go out there and be good, be absolutely AMAZING. Be yourself and let spirituality find you. It's your choice and you can achieve anything want to. It's taking that first step on the road to success, so place your foot down and start walking. It's your choice of course, not mine.

DON'T QUIT

When things go wrong, as they sometimes will.

When the road you're trudging seems all uphill.

When the funds are low and the debts are high, and you want to smile, but you have to sigh.

When care is pressing you down a bit, rest, if you must, but don't you quit.

Life is queer with its twists and turns, as every one of us sometimes learns.

And many a failure turns about, when we might have won had we stuck it out.

Don't give up though the pace seems slow – you may succeed with another blow.

Often the goal is nearer than it seems to a faint and faltering man.

Often the struggler has given up, when he might have captured the victor's cup, and learned too late when the night slipped down, how close he was to the golden crown.

Success is failure turned inside out – the silver tint of the clouds of doubt, and you never can tell how close you are.

It may be near when it seems so far, so stick to the fight when you're hardest hit.

It's when things seem worst that you **MUST NOT QUIT**.

Author unknown

May your God, Guides, Healers, Guru's or whatever you would like to call them always be with you, walking beside you in life, always guiding you forward?

Thank you and kind regards **ALWAYS.**

Mike. (PSTEC Master Practitioner)

Morecambe Hypnotherapy Centre.

Change your beliefs and you will change your inner world.

Give PSTEC a try today.

Get your free download at: **www.mwhypno.co.uk** drop me a line letting me know how you're finding the PSTEC system. I will try my best to reply to as many people as I can, but if I don't get chance, don't be offended. It will possibly be due to time restraints.